Brain Games
for Your Child

Brain Games
for Your Child

Robert Fisher

SOUVENIR PRESS

First published in 2011 by Souvenir Press Ltd
43 Great Russell Street, London WC1B 3PD

ISBN 978-0-28564-043-6

Typeset by M Rules

Printed and bound in Great Britain

Acknowledgements

The author wishes to thank Julie Winyard and Dot and Stuart Childs for help in improving this book, and the teachers and children who helped his research into games for thinking and learning. The book is dedicated to the memory of his parents who first introduced him to family games.

Contents

Introduction

'A good game gets your brain going' child, aged 7

Your child is an amazing bundle of possibilities, with a mind and brain different from every other person. Nothing in nature is as complex or wonderful as your child's brain and you will really enjoy helping him make the most of it.*

Playing the games in this book can help boost your child's brain, build his confidence and stimulate his thinking. They will provide hours of fun, helping you to get to know him better, and helping him develop into a bright, happy and successful child.

Your child's amazing brain

A human brain is the most complex object we know of in the universe. Babies are born with billions of brain cells (also called neurons). But it is not the number of brain cells that determines their success in life but the *connections* between those cells. Thinking takes place when cells connect up within the brain. It is these individual patterns of connections that makes every brain different.

Children are born with enough brain cells to lead a successful life. Some of these cells are connected together or 'wired' before

*Note: In this book your child is referred to as him. The word 'him' refers to 'him' or 'her'.

birth, but more connections are made throughout childhood through the process of learning. Learning helps to organise and reorganise the connections within the brain. What is important is not the number of cells but the strength of the connections between them. It is the number and strength of these connections that builds brain power.

Your child's intelligence develops when his brain is stimulated to make connections. Brain scans show the difference between a brain that has been stimulated and a brain that is not stimulated (see fig). That's where you help – giving your child experiences that stimulate his thinking to make more connections in his brain. Playing brain games will help boost his brain in ways that you will both enjoy.

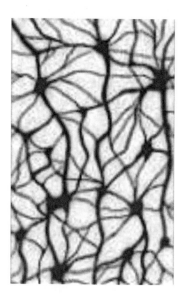
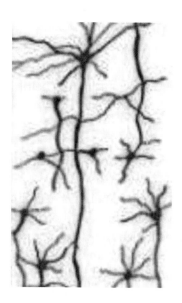

Fig 1a A stimulated brain   *Fig 1b An unstimulated brain*

A brain that is stimulated develops a rich network of connections that enables thinking and learning to take place. But these connections will need to be strengthened through practice. A child needs to repeat experiences, like climbing up steps or playing a game, to learn how to do it well. The more he practices the better he will become. As the connections get stronger so will his skill and confidence. That is why he will often want to play a favourite game, or hear a favourite story, over and over again. As one child said to me: 'You get better playing it again – and you get more chances of winning!'

A young child will do most of his learning at home with his parents and carers, not in the nursery, playgroup or school. His future success will be built on the foundation of his early learning experiences. Creating a happy learning environment will mean putting in effort but that effort will bring you satisfaction and the more fun it is the more you will look forward to playing together. Remember that playing brain games is not about creating a 'hothouse' environment by putting pressure on you or your child. It is about stimulating your child's ability to think by playing games that are fun and also develop his intelligence.

What does your child's brain need?

We know a lot about what helps to make brains work better. Here for example there are six things that a brain needs to function well. These are:

- food
- drink
- oxygen
- exercise
- rest
- stimulus

The brain works best when body is fit and healthy. It is a hungry organ, the hungriest in the human body. It needs food, drink and fresh air (oxygen) to function well. Encourage him to have plenty of exercise such as dancing, crawling, turning, balancing, climbing, stretching, running and jumping so that there is good blood flow to the brain. Every day should be an exercise day because gym for the body is also good for the brain.

Feed him on healthy foods and drinks, make sure he has plenty of fresh air, and ensure he has good periods of rest and sleep. Make sure he gets the mental stimulus his brain needs. Make every day a thinking day – by playing brain games!

No other species continues to play games for as long as humans do. Your child needs to play games and the best games are 'brain games'. A game becomes a 'brain game' when it challenges him to think and to solve problems. A game is not a 'brain game' when it is effortless, mindless and repetitive. Brain games challenge a child to think about what they are doing. And to play well he needs the help of others – his parents, friends and carers, who will help him play and stimulate his thinking.

How will this book help?

There are more than 200 games in this book, divided into four sections that cover the first all-important decade of your child's life. Stage one is 0–3 years, stage two is 3–6 years, stage three is 6–9 years and stage four is 9 years and older.

1 Brain Games 0–3 years
2 Brain Games 3–6 years
3 Brain Games 6–9 years
4 Brain Games 9+ years

Children vary in the way their minds and bodies develop. Some by the age of 6 can play games suitable for children of 9 or more years, others prefer to play games suitable for younger children (boys are usually less physically and mentally developed than girls of the same age). So your child may enjoy playing games from more than one stage in the book.

This book includes old favourites as well as unfamiliar games. What is common to all the games is that they depend on human beings not gadgets, machines or electronic equipment. They are about getting your child to talk and play with others rather than sitting in front of a machine. Electronic games are enjoyable and can be useful in getting him to think quickly but they generally rely on a narrow range of abilities. Prolonged exposure to quick-fire computer games can be harmful by enforcing a short-term attention span. Unlike the brain games in this book computer games may not encourage him to think, to talk with others or to concentrate for any length of time. The games here need only simple materials that are easily available and people for him to play and communicate with. These games will encourage him to pay attention and help develop a wide range of abilities, including his language and number skills.

What skills do the games develop?

Playing these games will encourage your child to talk as well as think. As Joe, a nine year old said: 'You have to be good at talking if you want to be good at thinking.' On each games page are listed the main skills developed by those games. As well as speaking and listening, these skills include:

- Concentration – paying attention, observing and thinking carefully
- Logical thinking – making decisions that are based on reasons and logic
- Creative thinking – using imagination and coming up with new ideas

- Strategic thinking – thinking ahead and assessing the consequences of decisions
- Problem solving – tackling problems and overcoming obstacles
- Language skills – developing vocabulary, reading, writing and other linguistic skills
- Mathematical skills – developing understanding of number and geometrical shapes
- Visual thinking – developing understanding of visual shapes, images and drawings
- Social skills – co-operating with others, playing by rules, winning and losing with grace

Concentration is needed if your child is to follow rules, solve problems and learn new things. It is a skill that often does not come naturally and needs to be practised. Help him to pay attention so that he makes the most of the games you play. Point things out to him, say things that will interest and enthuse him. Praise him for his efforts to work things out.

Solving problems requires many kinds of thinking – logical thinking, creative thinking, strategic thinking, planning and decision-making. For example *Boxes* (see p78) is a simple two-player game that has each player alternately drawing lines between dots on a sheet of paper to create boxes. To play well you need to think ahead about the consequences of what you do. When I played one of my sons and lost it reminded me once again of the importance of concentrating on the game!

Many of the games require players to talk to each other. The more he plays with words and sounds the greater success your child will have in learning to read and write. The same is true of mathematical skills. The more your child plays with numbers, keeps scores, for example through dice games (see p86), and learns about shapes through playing with them (see p30) the more you are helping him to prepare for mathematical challenges at school.

Visual thinking is equally important. More than half of human brain activity is taken up by processing what one sees. Understanding pictures, images and drawings is an essential skill in the modern world. The artist Paul Klee described drawing as taking a line for a walk. Your child may not become a great artist like Klee, but by practising drawing he will get better and more confident at it. By playing drawing games (see p77) you will help develop his drawing and visual skills. Try taking some paper and crayons in your pocket when out with a young child so he can draw with them when he is having to stop or wait.

Social skill and confidence is developed through playing games with others, as well as the ability to cope with conflicting emotions. As one child put it: 'I want to play and I don't want to play because I hate losing!' The self-discipline that comes from the ability to control ones emotions and to understand the emotions of others (what experts call emotional intelligence) is vital to success in life. Help him to understand and control his emotions – it is more important than getting a right answer or winning a game.

You will find a list of games at the end of the book. Choose a game and start playing!

How to play the games

1 Teaching a new game

Make sure everyone knows how to play before you start. If you have played the game before ask your child to remind you (and other players) what the rules are.

When teaching your child a new game remember to:

- speak facing towards your child, making frequent eye contact
- use simple words, keep sentences short and repeat what is important

- add gestures to help explain the game, and point out specific objects and events
- check that your child understands what you are explaining
- ask him to explain the game and invite him to ask questions
- talk about the game as you play and show you are enjoying it
- don't worry if he does not want to play, try another time or another game

Share with him your favourite games, learn what he enjoys playing and experience once more the pleasures of childhood.

2 Choosing who plays first

Once everyone knows how to play you need to decide who starts the game. There are many ways to choose who plays first, for example:

- give the youngest player the chance to play first
- the player on the left of the dealer starts
- ask which player(s) wants to begin
- toss a coin
- throw a die (highest score goes first)
- pick a playing card (highest ranked card goes first)
- ask players to choose which hand you have hidden an object in

Whoever begins give other players a chance to go first in other rounds. Once a game has started play usually continues with the next player on the left, in a clockwise direction.

3 Playing the game

There is no one right way to play a game, so vary or adapt them, and play them in your own way. If a game is not working then change the rules to make it easier or more interesting. Play in a way that suit you and your child best!

Give your child some clues as to the best strategy to win, by asking for example: 'What happens if you do this . . . ?' or 'What do you need to remember to try to do?' After you have played the game discuss with your child how it was played.

Watch for signs that your child is tired or bored with the game. Be ready to have a rest from playing or try playing something different or take turns with your partner in playing a game. Maybe mum, or one partner, plays one night and dad or the other partner the next. Try to involve all of your child's carers in playing these games.

Conclusion

Playing with you will make the games more interesting for your child and you will have the reward of knowing that you are not only boosting his brain but are creating bonds and memories that will last a lifetime. So whenever you can – play up and play the game!

1

Brain Games for babies (0–3 years)

Your baby is born with a brain that contains all the elements of human intelligence. What he needs is help in developing this intelligence.

New born babies recognise their mother's voice but find it hard to focus their eyes or make much sense of the world in the first two or three months. They find out about the world largely through their eyes but their focus is limited to 8–10 inches (20–25cms) and anything nearer or further away appears blurred. After about 6 weeks the eyes focus but he will remain short-sighted for sometime after that. He starts by recognising faces, then gradually begins to see and understand the world around him. Help in this process of development by playing games from birth, such as *Look at this, Watch it move* and *Peepo!* (see Games 1–9).

Talk to your baby as you play with him. Respond to his infant coos with delighted replies. Repeat your syllables slowly in a high-pitched voice when you say 'Look at this!' or 'Clever baby!' Speak slowly with a singsong or up-down quality and a slightly higher pitch as it holds your baby's attention longer than the ordinary way of speaking. Experts call this way of talking 'parentese'.

By the age of three months a healthy baby takes increasing charge of its environment. It skilfully manipulates the behaviour of its mother and other caregivers so that it gets the attention, care and food it needs through a mixture of gaze, facial expression and voice (by crying). His brain develops through play and interaction with others. He will be fascinated by objects that move or make a noise, so hanging mobiles over where a baby is lying helps their visual interest and development. After three months introduce your child to new kinds of games (see Games 10–15).

Babies from one month often produce their first 'ooh' sounds from pleasurable experiences like play. Understanding what others say gradually develops from about 6 months. From 6 to 9 months babies can repeat vowel sounds like 'dadadada' which begin to sound like speech. Help by 'guessing' what he is trying to say. His first words are usually spoken after a year, with a burst of new words coming about the middle of the second year as he increasingly repeats what he hears. Talking to your child and encouraging him to respond can really help in his language development.

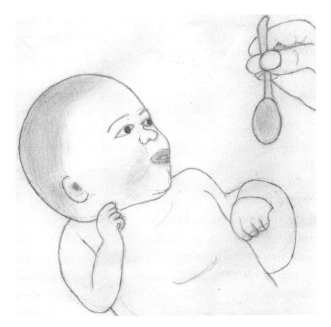

Fig 2 Baby watching held object

Play story games, singing games, rhyming games, action games, musical games, drawing games and other active games to develop your child's growing range of skills (for a list of skills see p5–6). These brain games, including pretend play will help prepare him for the next stage of development beginning around the age of three (see Games 15–30).

Brain Games for babies 0–3 years

1 Look at this!
2 Watch it move!
3 Peepo!
4 Sounds funny
5 Funny faces
6 Music making
7 Talk talk
8 Get that rhythm!
9 Touchy feely games
10 Surprise package
11 Take it out and put it back
12 Happy clap and finger rhymes
13 Finger and sock puppets
14 Play dough
15 Sort it out
16 Coming alive
17 Painting fun
18 Stories about me
19 Baby books
20 Puzzle shapes and pictures
21 Treasure hunts
22 Simon says
23 Build a tower
24 Pretend play

1 Look at this!   *Age 0–18 months*

Collect everyday items from around the house and show him two or three new ones every few days. Try to choose colourful and boldly patterned objects and things that you can make a noise with. Hold the object about a foot (30cm) from his face and ask him 'What's this?' Allow him time to explore the look of each object. Tell him what the object is and what you can do with it. Leave a display of two or three objects hanging above his cot so he can see and explore them in his own time.

- **Crib gym**
  Give him a crib gym to play with. You can make a crib gym by hanging brightly coloured objects from a secure cord or rod across his crib to stimulate his senses. He will begin by looking at bright interesting things, and later want to touch, strike, bat or swipe them with his hands.

- **Look at this!**
  Show your baby something and tell him what it is, for example: 'Look at this! It's a spoon!'. Remember to talk very slowly and clearly to him. He will not understand what you say but he will be learning about the sounds of talk and also about things in his strange new world.

- **What's this?**
  Look at baby books together, for example books made of cloth
  or thick board. Choose books with simple clear pictures of
  everyday objects, point to a picture and say 'What's this?' And
  then talk to him about it and try to show him a real-life object
  that matches the picture.

- **Look at the light!**
  Carry your baby into a dark room and sit on a chair or floor.
  Turn on a flashlight and say 'Look at the light!' Slowly move
  the light around focusing on various objects, such as pictures
  or toys, and say what they are. If your baby is afraid of the
  dark, leave the door open or turn on a dim night light. Never
  shine the light in your baby's eyes.

Key skills: Develops eye and brain co-ordination, listening and
early language skills.

2 Watch it move!   *Age 0–1*

Once he can follow movement with his eyes play 'Watch it
move!' Fix a little toy to a stick then move it from side to side,
so he can follow it with his eyes, then try up and down, in and
out and other directions.

- **Watch it move!**
  As he gains control of his head prop it up on some cushions
  then try to show him all the ways things can move – blow
  bubbles, play with balloons, roll and bounce balls, then show
  how balls can knock skittles down.

- **Bat a mobile**
  Give him a mobile he can bat with his fingers. Hang the items
  about 30cm from your babies eyes on the right or left of the

crib At first he will look at it and not touch it. Later he will learn to suck it and bat it with his hand.

- **Chew-a-book**
  When your child is about 4 months old give him some good thick card books. He will then learn not only how to chew books but also learn how to turn the pages. The chewing will help his gums and the page-turning, long before he can read, will teach him that books are fun and pages can be moved.

- **Give it to me**
  Play a 'give it to me' game. Hold a soft toy just out of his reach and move it so that it 'dances' in front of him. If your baby makes a sound or moves in response give it to him. 'Here you are. You can play with . . .' Then hold your hand out and say: 'Give it to me'.

- **Be a copy cat**
  Play copy cat games. Sit opposite your baby in his high chair. Give him a spoon. Take your own spoon and tap it on a tray. See if he copies what you do, if not take his hand and show him how to tap the spoon. Let him copy you wiggling your fingers, shaking your head, sticking your tongue out, touching ears, waving or clapping. Say what you are doing as you do it.

Later your baby will learn that objects exist not only when they move, but also when they are out of sight.

Key skills: Visual perception, hand and brain co-ordination

3 Peepo! *2–18 months*

Show your baby how things though out of sight can stay in his mind, by playing Peepo! (or Peek-a-boo!). Cover your eyes with

your hands, open them and cry 'Peepo!' or 'Boo!' Vary the game
by peeping from either side of your hands and by moving to different positions. Try turning your head away then suddenly back,
and hiding behind objects or furniture. He will soon learn to
anticipate your reappearance.

- **Peepo!**
  Put a scarf over your head and say: 'Where has mummy/daddy
  gone?' Wait a few seconds, quickly remove the scarf, saying
  'Peepo!' You can play 'Peepo' by hiding behind a chair, a door,
  the curtains or another person. Play 'Peepo' while doing various activities like housework, such as ironing or washing.
  Treat household chores as a chance to play Peepo games with
  your baby. Make some funny sounds while you do it.

- **Here it is!**
  Show your baby a toy, then hide it, for example under a blanket or behind your back asking 'Where did it go?' Pop it back
  out with a 'Here it is! It was under the cover/behind me!'
  Initially, it is better to be predictable so your baby can anticipate the toy's reappearance. Then try popping the toy up
  from some strange locations!

- **Where has it gone?**
  Hide a small object in one hand and play 'Which hand is it
  in?' A variation is to put a grape under a cup and say: 'Where
  has it gone?' then lift the cup and say: 'There it is!' Later,
  when he is about one, try hiding a grape under one of two
  cups. Then ask where it has gone. Then see if your child can
  hide an object under a cup for you.

Play other hiding games such as hiding toys under a cloth, and
ask 'Where is Teddy hiding?'

Key skills: Develops perceptual, memory, predictive and problem solving skills.

4 Sounds funny   *2 months on*

Find things that make funny sounds such as rattles, bells, paper, glass objects or tin cans. Make sounds from different positions, for example shake a small container of rice to his left and then his right. Wait for him to look to find the source of the noise.

The funniest sounds may come from your voice. Humans can make a greater variety of sounds than any other animal. Your child can make any sound in any human language if he is encouraged. Test this out by making some funny sounds and see if he copies you.

- **Funny sounds**
  Try saying some simple high sounds such as 'Wheeee!' and some low sounds such as 'Oooooh!' Call him or make some funny sounds from different parts of the room, from low down and high up, encouraging him to track your voice. See how many different funny sounds you can make?

The next time your baby gives you a prod make a funny noise, like 'buzz'. He'll probably try again, so repeat the sound every time he prods you. After some time try a different sound such as 'boop', 'beep' or 'pop' and pull a funny face. End the game by saying for example: 'You made me 'buzz'/'boop'/'beep'. What a clever boy!' Vary the game by making different animal noises. Try seeing what noises your baby might want to make when you prod him.

Key skills: Listening, voice and pre-language skills

5 Funny faces   *2 months on*

Nothing is as interesting to a baby as a human face. He will smile at crude face patterns, such as two dots on a card, so draw some funny faces for him to look at. By eight weeks he will prefer real faces but may still smile at drawings.

By four months he will probably only smile at faces he knows. Amuse him not only by drawing but also by pulling some funny faces and by making funny sounds as you do. Try different facial expressions and sounds to develop your baby's vision and hearing. Here are some ideas: blink your eyes, stick out your tongue; cough or yawn; sing a song using big lip movements; make contortions with your mouth, poke your tongue out, waggle your ears and shake your head. Encourage him to mimic them.

- **Mirror games**
  From about 6 months hold him on your lap with a mirror. Ask him 'Who is that in the mirror?' show him that when he moves his reflection moves too, and that the funny face in the mirror is you! Give him a mirror to play with in his playpen.

- **Funny faces**
  As your child grows older, show him pictures of funny faces in books and magazines. Say what the face looks like eg 'sad', 'happy', 'old' and try to pull a similar kind of face yourself.

Older children can start enjoying and making their own face masks.

Key skills: face recognition, perceptual and language skills.

6 Counting games   *2 months on*

Begin counting games by saying 'one, two' when you are doing regular routines such as putting arms or legs into clothes or rocking him in your arms. Then go on to 'one, two, three' games, for example:

- **One, two, three up!**
  This is a fun baby game that will help anticipation skills as well as give your baby some exercise.
  1 Lie your baby down on a soft flat surface such as the bed or blanket on the carpet.
  2 Hold on to your baby's hands and wrists then count, 'One, two, three, Up!'
  3 Gently pull your baby up to a sitting position. Smile and lower your baby back to the lying position then repeat.
  4 After several repetitions your baby will anticipate the ride up. Alter the count to add variation.

Key skills: Anticipation, memory,

7 Making Music   *2 months on*

A young child was making an awful banging sound with a spoon on tins in the kitchen. 'What is that noise?' I shouted. 'It's only Tom,' replied my wife, 'he's composing his first piece of music!' Babies love making a noise. Encourage him as much as your nerves can stand, with some instruments that make musical sounds. Give him a rattle as soon as he can grasp, for example a plastic bottle with a screw top filled with beans and other things that make a sound that he can shake.

- **Bang the drum**
  After about 6 months, give him different kinds of 'drums' to hit, such as a saucepan with a wooden spoon. Play him music on your CD player so that he can bang and shout along.

- **Listen to this**
  Let him hear sounds made for example as by dropping different objects such a pan lid, wooden brick or small bell. Talk about and listen to natural sounds like a clock ticking, bird song, phone sounds, animal sounds, weather sounds, tap dripping and water splashes.

Encourage your child to listen to sounds around you and to sounds as you make them – clapping, tapping, banging, stamping, blowing, crying, laughing, scraping and so on and talk about the sounds he can hear (see also Musical Jars p64)

Key skills: Listening, music and language skills

7 Talk talk   *2 months–3 years*

The sound that babies prefer more than any other is the sound of speech. They turn to you when you speak and you keep your baby's brain active by talking. They turn to hear where the sound of speech, such as on the radio or TV, is coming from.

- **Talk about it**
  Talk to your baby all the time and everywhere. At bath-time touch and name each part of his body as you wash it. As you dress your child talk about the clothes you are putting on. As you cook or clean talk about what you are doing. Tell your baby some tales, you can even tell him your troubles knowing the sounds you make will be doing him some good.

It does not matter if your baby cannot understand what you are saying, he will learn speech if you do not talk to him, but he will learn it quicker if you do.

- **Create conversation**
  A conversation can be a kind of game that you try to keep going with your child. From about 18 months when he learns to talk, build on his language by trying to create a new conversation every day. Use whole sentences, and keep the conversation going by asking questions and making up stories.

Invite him to become part of the game. Try to turn whatever he says into a conversation. For example if your child says 'There's a cat' say for example 'Yes, look at its a shiny black coat and long whiskers' 'Does it look like grandma's cat?' 'Do you remember when we saw that snowy white cat?' or 'I wonder what the cat is thinking?'

Key skills: Connecting ideas, stimulating imagination, developing language skills

8 Get that rhythm! *2 months on*

Sharing rhythms and rhymes with your baby will help boost his language skills. All babies respond to rhythm. The first rhythm he is aware of is his mother's heartbeat. Before he can talk the rhythm of speech can be heard in his babbling. He will love rhythmical movement, being rocked, rhythmical sounds like rhymes and rhythmical music like lullabies. Bounce your baby on your knee in time to music or a favourite song, or hold him in your arms and dance with him around the room. Give him some rhythm!

- **Nursery rhyme song and dance**

  Nursery rhymes mimic the rhythms of speech. So say and sing some nursery rhymes regularly to your baby. Rock him, or dance with him in your arms, in time to the words that you say or sing.

- **Action rhymes**

  At about 6 months you can start adding actions to words, at about a year he will be able to join in with actions to rhymes such as 'The wheels on the bus go round and round'. If you are too busy to sing songs or say rhymes then buy a CD for your baby to listen to.

From the age of two put actions to the rhythm of nursery rhymes. Start with familiar spoken rhymes like 'Humpty Dumpty' and move on to action songs like 'Here we go round the mulberry bush'. Encourage them to sing the words with you to help them keep to the rhythm.

A good example of an action song is:

This is the way the ladies ride	
Trip trop, trip trop, trip trop.	Bounce baby up and down on your knee.
This is the way the gentlemen ride	
Gall-op, gall-op, gall-op.	Bounce slower but more vigorously.
This is the way the farmer rides	
Hobble-dee, hobble-dee.	Bounce baby from side to side
And down in the ditch!	Open legs and let baby slide down.

Key skills: Rhythmic, musical, prediction, listening and language skills

9 Touchy feely games   *2 months on*

Give your baby different objects to touch. Put into his hands
objects that feel different; hard, soft, firm, squashy, silky, coarse,
cold, warm, wet, dry, smooth, furry – anything he can safely
handle. A baby's fist does not fully relax until one month after
birth. Help him to hold things. Begin by putting your fingers
in his grasp. Later place rattles and small toys in his hands (make
sure that none of the things you give him can be swallowed).

- **Hold it**
  After 6 months or so many babies can grasp a wide variety of
  objects, such as plastic toys or cups, lids, rings and any clean
  materials he might like to chew. Beware of small objects he
  might swallow or newsprint which may be toxic. Put him on
  different surfaces and draw attention to different textures and
  how they feel to the touch.

- **Scribble scribble**
  From about 12 months most infants can hold a crayon in their
  fist and start scribbling. If encouraged most children by 15
  months can scribble up and down and by 21 months round
  and round. Give him large pieces of paper to develop his scribbling skills. This lays the foundation for future writing skills.

- **Mystery objects**
  With children aged 2 or 3 put 'mystery objects' into a bag
  and see if he can guess what each one is by feeling it. Get him
  to describe what he is feeling. Make a 'mystery box' by cov-
  ering a cardboard box with wrapping paper, with holes on
  each side so your child can put both hands in the box. Fill the
  box with mystery objects. The object of the game is to
  describe and name each object, then pull it out to see if he is
  correct.

Key skills: Manipulative skills, tactile awareness and hand-eye co-ordination.

10 Surprise package   *6 months on*

Children of all ages are incredibly curious. And *surprise package* is a game that they will really enjoy. Start by showing him how you hide a toy under a cloth and then show him how to find it. Wrap a little toy in 3 or 4 layers of paper, just fold the paper don't stick it. Then get him to unwrap it. Repeat the game with different wrappings and a different surprise toy each time.

- **Hide a toy**
  From 1 year on you can show him how to *hide a toy* under a towel and see if he can create his own surprise. From about two children can learn to open their own surprise package presents.

- *Magic scarf box*
  Stimulate your baby's curiosity with an empty tissue box and some lightweight, colourful scarves or cloths.
  1 Tie the scarves together (end to end) then place them in the empty tissue box. Leave one small end of a scarf out, enough to tickle your baby's interest.
  2 Get your baby's attention and start to pull out the scarf line saying, 'Look at what I found, now you try it!' Offer him the scarf and hopefully see him start to pull. As he gets older, you can also teach him how to put the scarves back in the tissue box to start again.
  You can also try using an empty cardboard tube instead of the tissue box. Be sure to never leave your baby alone with the line of tied scarves or he may get tangled.

- **Pass the parcel**

  From about three he will be able to play *'pass the parcel'* games.

  1 Wrap a present in many layers of paper to create a surprise package, lightly sealed with tape.
  2 Play music, while children pass the parcel in turn to each other.
  3 When the music stops the child with the parcel unwraps one, and only one, layer.
  4 The child who takes the last layer off wins the game (and the prize).

  The game is a good lesson in turn-taking and sharing.

Key skills: Problem-solving, perceptual and manipulative skills.

11 Take it out and put it back   *6 months on*

Babies and toddlers love filling and emptying things. Find containers such as an old box or drawer and fill it up with interesting objects and toys. He will find it easier to take things out than to put them back, a trait that lasts a lifetime!

- **'I've dropped it in the water!'**

  Challenge him to finding something you have dropped into the water.

- **Lucky dip**

  From about 12 months fill a carton with screwed up paper and hide a toy in it for him to find.

- **Sandpit games**

  Introduce him to a sandpit from about one year and a choice of equipment like spades, spoons, buckets, cups sieve or colander and moulds with which to make shapes. This will provide hours of fun and develop understanding of the behaviour of fluid substances and use of tools.*

- **Shaving foam hunt**
  When your child is three try a container full of shaving foam with objects hidden inside. Get him to describe the objects before pulling them out so that you can guess what they are.

Once your baby can take things out and put them back into a box, try the game with containers with lids and containers with different compartments and shape sorters.

Key skills: Develops hand/eye co-ordination and hand manipulation. Knowing that objects are there even when not seen promotes thinking and language skills.

12 Happy clap and finger rhymes   *1 year on*

When your baby can use both hands together you can play clapping games, like 'pat-a-cake', by clapping and patting the baby's palms alternately. The rhythmic repetition of rhyming words helps language development, clapping can help develop hand/eye co-ordination and rhythmic knowledge.

- **'Teddy Bear's garden'**
  Say *'Round and round the garden like a teddy bear'* (while circling your child's palm with your finger). *'One step'* (move finger up child's lower arm). *'two steps, and . . .'* (step finger up to upper

*For your sandpit use fine quality silver sand, not builders sand. An outdoor pit should be securely covered against rain and animals like cats who will use it as a litter tray. Sand play does not have to be outdoors. A box, or an old tyre on a plastic sheet can serve just as well – or even just a bowl of sand can be fun to play with.

arm). *'Tickle him under there!'* (tickle under child's arm). Tickling games can be fun from 6 weeks on.

Try more elaborate finger rhymes when your baby can move each finger independently. A good game is the 'foxy' rhyme:

- **Foxy's finger rhyme**
  'Put your finger in the foxy's hole' (guide his finger between the middle fingers of your clenched fist). *'Foxy's not at home! Foxy's out the back . . .'* (keep his finger trapped and open out your palm). *'Chewing on a bone!'* (Chew baby's finger).

Get a book of finger rhymes from a bookshop or library and encourage him to copy your gestures, using all his fingers.

Key skills: Develops hand/eye co-ordination and pre-writing skills

13 Finger and sock puppets   *12–18 months*

Ready-made *finger puppets* can be bought. They can also be simply made out of paper with a little cap taped to fit over the end of your finger with a face and hair drawn, stuck or sewn on. Pretend your finger puppet is a real person to talk to and play with. Make two puppets and hold a conversation or a dance or play hide and seek with each other. Later try making a puppet for your baby's finger.

- **Sock puppets**
  From about 20 months introduce him to *sock puppets*. They can be bought or made from felt or an old sock with eyes and lips sown on. The mouth can be between thumb and fingers. Show him what the puppet can do, for example speak, sing,

wave, pick up things, or pinch noses. Give your puppet a funny voice and if you make one for either hand get them to say things to each other. You can also use your finger or sock puppet as a character from a story you are reading to him. See p31

- **Spoon puppets**
  Make a *wooden spoon puppet* by drawing a face on a wooden spoon and wrapping some cloth around the handle.

- **Paper plate puppets**
  Paper plates can also make good puppet faces. Use marker pens to draw a face on each plates showing a different feeling – smiling, sleeping, surprised, crying, laughing, sad, angry, yawning and so on. Hold each plate up and mimic the expression, saying for example: 'Here is Jane. She is feeling sad. I wonder why she is feeling sad?' Make up a little story with two or more puppets, for example: 'Jane is sad because Ben took her toy. Let's ask for it back.'

Puppet play like this will help your child understand the feelings of others and therefore be better able to understand his own (see also Pretend Play p40)

Key skills: Develops imagination, understanding of others, language and finger skills.

14 Play dough   *18 months–3 years*

You can buy play dough or similar modelling materials from shops, but it is cheaper and more fun to make your own.

- **Play dough**
  Take 2 cups of flour, one cup of salt and one cup of water to make the basic dough. Add a spoonful of oil to make it feel smoother, and add colour to make it look more interesting. Knead it together and warm gently in a pan until it forms a soft lump. Give it to your child to play with when it is still warm. Show him how different shapes can be made by pulling, pushing and tearing it apart. As he grows older give him different tools such as blunt knives, shape cutters, small pots, rolling pins, shape stamps and wooden blocks to help work the play dough.

Children usually prefer to push, squeeze, roll and pound it rather than model it into realistic objects. Use pastry cutters to make different shapes, flatten into biscuits to bake in make-believe ovens. Challenge your child to make a ball or by rolling it out to make a long skinny snake. Both a ball or snake shape can easily become a dough animal, pet or monster. You can re-use your play dough if it is kept it in a plastic bag in the fridge.

Play dough can also be used to make number and letter shapes. It is also a good preparation for learning to cook.

Key skills: Develops language and manipulative skills, mathematical and scientific knowledge about shape and weight.

15 Sort it out   *15 months on*

Learning to name objects means learning how to identify and classify things – essential skills of language, science and maths. Help your young child to sort and classify things for it is the basis of future learning.

- **Sort the animals**
  Make a collection of plastic animals, with at least two kinds of each animal. Pick up an animal and say: 'Find me an animal like this', for example show him a sheep and see if he can find a sheep to match. If after a while he cannot find a matching animal give him some help. Repeat the game with different animals. After about 18 months see if he can sort out all the animals into pairs and into different types. Say the name of each animal.

- **Have a sort out**
  Play with objects of different colours, for example saying; 'Find me things that are blue.' Sorting vegetables can be fun too. Begin for example by asking him to separate the potatoes from the carrots. Try the same game with all kinds of things, such as bricks of different shapes or a collection of socks.

- **Sort the nuts from the bolts**
  Fill a jar with two sorts of objects, such as nuts and bolts, long and short screws or small and large coins. Pour out the objects onto a cloth. Ask your child to sort out two kinds of object, and put them into different boxes or cartons. Then ask him to try sorting three, four, five or six kinds of object from around the house such as coins, beads, cut-up coloured straws or dried beans.

- **Match the shapes**
  Extend basic sorting games by *matching shapes*, for example use three identical bricks to make different patterns. Ask him to make the same pattern. Show him if necessary and see if he can copy your patterns.

Sorting games helps your child to classify things and make choices about what goes together.

Key skills: Classification, logic and language skills

16 Coming alive   *1 year on*

Do you remember as a child when you pretended your favourite cuddly toy was alive? The ability to imagine and pretend is gradually learned in his second year. In stimulating his imagination you enable him to think beyond what he can actually do when playing for example with toys, simple dolls or cars.

- *Teddy comes to life*
  Help him playing with a teddy or cuddly toy by talking to his teddy, pretending he responds and by making him walk, go to sleep, eat or drink. Say what you are doing with teddy and what teddy is saying to you. By helping him to pretend you are helping him to develop his imagination, to put himself in someone else's shoes and to become aware that others have needs and feelings.

- **Pretend to . . .**
  Show him how to pretend for example to drink from a toy cup, or use a toy phone to phone someone. Gradually he will copy you and learn how to pretend.

- **A story come to life**
  Stories in books can be used to start pretend games. Pretend to be scared of a picture monster in a story book, or to eat the picture of a cake. Talk to the characters in the book and respond to what they do. Puppets are also great for pretend play (see p40)

Key skills: Develops imagination, awareness of others and language skills.

17 Painting fun   *20 months on*

Get some paint and a brush and show your young child how to brush colour onto paper (or onto a wall that you are decorating). Give him a little bucket of water or thin paint, find a suitable wall, fence or large piece of paper, give him a thick brush and let him have a splash with the paint. If nothing else it will give him a feeling of success. He can say to himself 'I made that mark.' He can pretend he is decorating or making a colourful picture. Who knows one day he may be a great artist – or house decorator.

- **Painting fun**
  Give him a thick brush and some scrap paper. Dress him in an apron and set up a 'messy' corner. Show him how to put paint on paper by splodging it on, flicking, wiping, trickling it on and using fingers. Then leave him to experiment. Making a mess is part of the fun.

- **Comb and paste patterns**
  Mix some wallpaper paste with your paints. Splash it onto paper and show your child how to swirl it round into interesting patterns with a comb, fingers or other tool

Remember two year olds are still at the stage of experimenting with paint rather than painting pictures, so don't say 'What is it?' Enjoy your child's experimental fun with colours. Try getting him to paint with fingers, feet, sponges, feathers, corks, sticks, marbles or string. A creative child can paint inside or outside of boxes, on cartons, rocks, balloons, walls and many other surfaces. Keep a good variety of paints to hand, ready for painting games.

From 3 years on you can introduce your child to printing.

Key skills: Develops hand manipulation, imagination and knowledge of cause and effect.

18 Stories about me   *20 months on*

Towards the end of the second year tell him some simple stories about his early life, for example 'This is your hat when you were a baby'. Photos are a great way in, for example: 'This was you when you were first born', 'This is you at the park', 'This is mummy when he . . .' As time goes on you can build these small bits of information into longer stories.

- **Body stories**
  You can help him learn more about himself by naming each part of his body, for example; 'This is your nose, this is your ear' and so on. Counting starts with your baby's body; 'You've got one nose, two ears and one, two, three, four, five toes.' Tweak each toe as you say 'One, two, three, four, five; once I caught a fish alive. Six, seven, eight, nine, ten; then I let it go again.'

- **Stories of the day**
  Remind your child of some of the highlights of his day, for example a shopping trip, visit of a friend, a game, relative, animal, what he saw, heard or had for breakfast. Share your child's stories to help him remember the story of his day, perhaps just after a bath or before bedtime. Tell him some stories about your day.

- **Stories about the past**
  Tell him stories about himself to remind him what happened in the past. A young child finds it hard to talk about things that are not there in front of him. Talking about events that

have happened helps him to picture the past and fix them in his memory. Later he will be able to remember events and tell you stories about himself.

Key skills: Understanding past and present, developing memory, language and number skills.

19 Baby books
12 weeks on

In spite of television and computers books still underpin much of our education, reading and language skills. Show picture books to your baby from about 6 weeks. Books with simple shapes and bold colours work best. Turn the pages for him (he will probably not be able to turn the pages himself until about 1 year).

- **Read baby books**
  There are many ways of sharing books. One is to give your child a book to look at and play with by himself. Another is to cuddle up with him beside you to share a book. Many parents and carers begin reading stories and rhymes to their child from soon after they are born (and some begin before birth!). Your baby may want you to reread a story several times. This really helps him retain what he has just heard. Try to make it fun for both of you!

- **Story sounds**
  Make book reading more enjoyable by encouraging him to join in with sound effects. Making sounds will give him a more vivid sense of the story, will teach him to anticipate what comes next and associate certain sounds with words. Invite him to join in and make his own fun sounds.

- **Make-a-book**
  Make books together about daily events by sticking in a blank book some photos of places you have visited and things you have seen or done.

Even though your baby does not understand the meaning behind the words he hears, it is still important to ask questions. Practice asking questions that require thinking, for example 'How will the rabbit escape?' and show your interest in whatever response he makes. By about 18+ months your baby will be better able to answer your questions and understand the meaning of words you have introduced.

Key skills: Language skills, memory, problem solving and imagination.

20 Puzzle shapes and pictures   *1–3 years*

By the end of the first year it will be time to introduce some simple puzzles. These may be bright shapes cut out of wood so that they can fit into the same shaped hole. At first try puzzles that only have two or three pieces at first, such as circle, triangle and square. Pieces with handles to hold on to are best. Stay with simple puzzles until your child is confident with them. It will teach him not only about shapes but also how to experiment when faced with a problem.

- **Jigsaw puzzles**
  Children can do simple jigsaw puzzles from about two years. Wooden jigsaw puzzles are best bought from a shop as you will need to be a skilled carpenter to make one that fits well. The first puzzles you buy should have about six or seven simple pieces. Picture puzzles provide good opportunities for

talking to your child about the shapes and to tell him stories about what the picture shows.

- **Card puzzles**
  Make your own simple jigsaw puzzles out of old Christmas cards or other cards with coloured pictures. Simply cut the picture up into a few different shapes and see if he can fit them back together. It is best if you have two picture cards the same, so one can be cut one up and the other kept whole as a model. Keep the pieces of each puzzle safe in an old envelope.

A good puzzle will keep a child quietly busy while he explores the pieces by himself. Commercial toys such as shape posting boxes and puzzle boards with small handles provide good practice in hand and eye co-ordination. Later he will be able to tackle more complex picture puzzles and jigsaws.

Key skills: Manipulation, shape awareness, memory and language skills.

21 Treasure hunts   *2 years on*

Ask your child to choose a bag or container from a selection you offer. Get him to take it along with you on a walk in the garden, to the park or nearby space. Make a game of 'looking for treasure'. This could be 'treasure' of any kind your child chooses, for example small stones or dead leaves. If he finds it difficult to choose suggest looking for something special like beautiful leaves.

- **Treasure hunt**
  You can play treasure hunt in your garden or indoors. For example hide a favourite toy somewhere in the room or garden

for your child to find. You can also play 'treasure hunt' with pictures, by saying for example: 'Can you find a dog in the picture?' or 'Where's the teddy?' The challenge of 'treasure hunts' outside is that your child has to look for and find some specific item. He must pick it up and put it in the bag or container. Later you talk about what has been found when you are back at home.

Treasure hunt is a good game to play on the beach or if you go for a walk in a wood. Show him how you can also paint or colour your treasures, for example stones once you get home if you want to. You can also play treasure hunt during special holidays e.g. find the Easter Egg or birthday surprise. With older children you can leave written clues that your child must follow around house and garden until he finds the 'hidden treasure'

Key skills: Close observation, fine finger control and language skills.

22 Simon says   *2 years on*

Physical co-ordination is an important brain function. These games will help develop your child's mind/body co-ordination:

- **Head, shoulders, knees and toes**
  A good mind/body co-ordination game for young children. To play it sing or chant these verses in a rhythmic manner:

  Head, shoulders, knees and toes,
  Knees and toes.
  Head, shoulders, knees and toes,
  Knees and toes and –
  Eyes and ears and mouth and nose.

Head, shoulders, knees and toes,
Knees and toes.

As you name each part of the body you, and your child, put your hand on the part mentioned. Try several times saying the verses quicker each time. Make up more verses naming different parts of the body, eg heels and nose; neck and toes.

- **Simon says**
  A favourite game for older children, though some children can learn to play it from the age of two. It is useful for physical co-ordination and learning parts of the body. It is best played with pairs or small groups of children.
  1 Start by saying 'Simon says . . . put your hands on your head' and demonstrate this. The children must copy you.
  2 Repeat 'Simon says' and introduce a different action, for example 'Simon says touch your toes/nose/ears/cover your eyes' etc. And the children must copy you to stay in the game.
  3 Then comes the tricky part. When you miss out 'Simon says' and simply say 'Put your hands on your head' and the child obeys he has lost the game and is 'out'. So children must look and listen carefully and co-ordinate their actions with you.

After playing a few times see if your child wants to try being Simon (or let them use their own name instead). Now you, or others, must follow what your child says as part of the game.

Key skills: Physical co-ordination, close observation, listening and language skills.

23 Build a tower   *2 years on*

Children love building towers. Given a collection of bricks or
stacking toys making a tower may seem a simple task, but it can
offer complex challenges to the budding builder. Use quality
wooden bricks if you can, for they will be made to scale so that
large bricks are in ratio to smaller bricks and arches and pillars
are matched in size to fit well together.

- **Build a tower**
  Start by giving your child a small number of bricks, just three
  or four to begin with. Show him how to put one brick on top
  of another. Build him a tower and let him have the fun of
  knocking it over. Let him experiment with a few bricks and
  don't expect progress to be quick. After a while give him more
  bricks and show him how to make a more stable tower with
  a base of four bricks.

When he is two he will simply pile up the bricks but by three
or four his building will become more precise and elaborate.
Through building with bricks he will absorb many basic mathematical and scientific principles. He will learn the value of
precision, the problems of balance, that some bricks are twice or
half the size of others, that round shapes roll, square shapes are
stable. He will not understand about area, volume and height or
the principles of engineering, but understanding these principles
will come more easily later if he has had some practical experiences of building with a range of construction materials.

- **Construction kits**
  Later he can be introduced to a range of commercial construction kits like Lego that will enable him to make a
  bewildering array of models.

If you make or mend things involve your child in the process. Children like to mimic adults and many a child has followed the model of a mum or dad who has made things.

Key skills: Manipulative, constructive, geometric and spatial skills.

24 Pretend play   *12 months on*

A young child needs to learn about feelings and words that describe feelings. So talk about your child's emotions and the emotions that others feel, both real people and pretend people that you read about in books or your child's toys, for example; 'Tom is feeling *happy* today.' 'Jane is *pleased* isn't he?' 'Ben is feeling *upset* because he fell over'

Children who do not know about the feelings of others, or who cannot express their own feelings in words, are more likely to resort to physical means in showing anger or frustration. It may take a long time for your child to understand his feelings. Begin by talking about them and teach him the words people use to describe what they feel.

- **Pretend play**
  Toys make good props when telling a story because they can move and be made to make the appropriate noises. Dolls, teddies and other soft toys are also ideal for pretend play and for talking about feelings. Through pretend play your child can act out what frightens, frustrates him, or makes him angry, for example the arrival of a new baby. Ask for example 'How is teddy feeling today?' or 'Teddy's hurt himself, let's make him better,' 'Teddy's dancing. He must be happy,' or 'Teddy's angry. What will help make him feel better?'

Pretend play allows your child to talk about his feelings by putting them on to a teddy or toy. This will help him understand what feelings are and how they can be controlled.

Key skills: Develops imagination, empathy (understanding of others) and language skills.

25 Musical stories

Long before speech develops, babies instinctively rock to music, clap their hands, bounce to the beat, and 'sing' along. Many studies have shown that music has a positive effect on children's learning. So try to build music into your child's play in ways he'll enjoy. Spontaneous music can come from everyday play such as gliding high on a swing and singing 'Up and down!' Sometimes the sounds around you can become the basis for rhythm and song, such as that dripping tap, weather sounds, machine noise or trains – so listen out, get into the rhythm and start to sing and soon your child will be joining in!

- **Musical stories**
  While reading a book, invite your child to create a rhythm for a character or event in the story. Introduce familiar, repetitive stories, such as *The Gingerbread Man* or *The House That Jack Built*. Invite your child to play some background music by humming or drumming on a pot, or to toot a horn when the main character enters a scene. For example, what would be the rhythm of the littlest Billy Goat tramping over the bridge in *Three Billy Goats Gruff*? How would the rhythm be different for the middle goat or the biggest goat?

- **Sing-a-long**

  Instead of reading a familiar nursery story sing it to your child. Never mind if it is not a great tune. The best songs are short and have repetitive words or lyrics and a limited note range. Vary the song by inviting your child to join in the singing or with hand movements. Listen to the songs your child is creating or the familiar tunes he's humming and reflect these in your choice of new songs to introduce. Make your own songbook of family favourites or classic songs such as 'My Hand Says Hello' (see below)

- **My hand says hello**

  'My Hand Says Hello' can be sung to the tune of 'The Farmer in the Dell' or your own tune. Ask your child to sing and show the different ways he can use his body to say hello: 'My hand says hello, My hand says hello. Every time I see my friend, My hand says hello.' Next verse: 'My (choose, or ask your child to choose another body part) says hello. . .'. . . and so on.

Key skills: Listening, language and musical skills.

26 Let's dance!

Moving begins with hands and arms and legs. Crawling leads to walking and walking leads to hopping, skipping, and jumping. When he hears music and it's hard for your child not to start moving in some way! Moving to music is how dance begins.

For many adults the word dance steps have a 'right' way to be done, but dance begins with simple natural and spontaneous movements and gestures. Exploring some simple dance movements with your child you will be helping to stimulate his musical and physical intelligence in ways that are fun. Make dance a regular expression of joy in living.

- **Can you move like this?**
  Encourage your child to experiment with moving his body.
  Say: 'Can you move like this?' Ask him 'Can you move
  another way?' Do a dance for your child with your hands and
  arms. Encourage him to explore the way his body moves using
  only his hands, arms, feet, or eyes.

- **Let's dance!**
  Put on different types of music, such as classical, pop, folk, or
  country. Say: 'Let's see how this music makes us feel.' Then
  invite your child to move freely to the music. Try introducing some props, such as scarves, balloons, paper fans, and
  feathers. Ask, 'How does this object make you want to move?'
  If you begin to dance he may well want to join you.

Key skills: Mind/body co-ordination, musical and physical
skills.

27 Bath time games   *18 months–3 years*

Bath time is a great opportunity to talk with your child and play
some brain games, such as showing your baby how water pours
in and out of different shaped containers and what toys float or
sink.

- **Float or sink?**
  Play these games in the bath or by setting up a small container filled with water next your baby. You will need several
  items that sink and several items that float. They should be
  small enough for your baby to pick up easily.
  1 With your baby in the bathtub (or next to the water filled
    container), put one of the floating items in the water and
    say, 'Look it floats!' Let your baby observe for a bit.

2 Next put a sinkable item in the water and say, 'It sinks!'
   Again, let him watch what happens.
3 Now repeat with other items, with some things that float
   and others that sink. Afterwards, let him pick and play
   with the objects himself.

As your baby gets older, try asking him which items will sink or
float – his answers may surprise you! Safety: remember never
leave your baby or toddler alone near or in the water

- **Bath time games**
  Try some of these quick games while he is in the bath:
  1 Wrap up a toy in a cloth and see if he can unwrap it.
  2 See if he can catch or trap a number of toys floating in the
    bath with a wooden spoon.
  3 Blow through a straw in the water and see if he can do it.
  4 Play filling and emptying various containers such as plas-
    tic spoons, yoghurt pots, plastic cups, bowls and bottles.
  5 Listen to different water sounds – dripping, bubbling,
    splashing etc and name the sound.
  6 Fill a sponge with water and squeeze it out into a container
    to see how much water it holds.
  7 Bathe and shampoo a doll or action figure, talking about
    different parts of the body, then dry it and put it to bed.

Key skills: Language, problem solving and maths skills (shape,
volume and capacity)

28 Obstacle Course   *8 months on*

Create an obstacle course for your baby. It can really help his
movement coordination and confidence while he learns to crawl

and walk. You will need an array of objects like pillows, boxes, blocks, or chairs to create an obstacle course.

He may begin by just going over or through objects on their way to you. Initially, you want to create a course of solid objects your baby cannot clamber over. Using natural barriers (walls, couches, chairs), create an obstacle course he must navigate around. Place him at the starting point then move to the end and call his name. When he navigates through the course – pick him and praise him. Help him by peeking around corners!

Begin the game in easy stages, starting for example with 'Through the Tunnel';

- **Through the Tunnel**
  1 Once he starts to crawl well make a small tunnel from a large cardboard box.
  2 Encourage him to crawl through the box to you as you wait at the far end.
  3 As he comes through the box say 'Boo!' and praise his success.

- **Obstacle course**
  An obstacle course is where he has to learn to climb over or go round various items to reach you. This will also help your baby to develop his awareness of height and balance. Start off easy so it is not too much of a challenge!
  1 You can create a line course by placing pillows and cushions of various heights between two solid barriers such as a couch and wall or boxes in a straight line.
  2 Place him at one end and then sit at the opposite end and call him over – encourage him to climb over each soft obstacle. Alternatively, you can create a pillow or cushion barrier around him, so he has to climb up and over to get to you.

Once your baby starts walking, you can create similar courses that encourage him to watch where he walks without tripping. This can be done by placing medium cubes and boxes on the floor for him to walk around. Similar obstacle courses can be made outside to challenge his physical and problem solving skills.

Key skills: Physical, problem solving, visual and memory skills

29 Hidden sounds   *2–3 years*

This game is like hide and seek with music. You will need a musical toy (electronic or windup) that your baby is familiar with and small enough to hide.

- **Hidden sounds**
  1 Start the musical toy and hide it under a sheet or blanket that will be fairly easy for your baby to hear and spot.
  2 Ask him, "Do you hear that? Where could the music be?" You may have to help him or crawl around with him to find it.
  3 Praise him when he uncovers the toy with a 'You found it, well done!' As he becomes better at finding the musical toy, you can hide it in more difficult to find places like under pillows, behind furniture or under the bed.

- **Hunt the Clock**
  Instead of a musical toy you could hide a ticking clock or buzzing mobile phone. Tell your child to listen very carefully. Give him clues as he begins his search, for example 'You are getting warmer!' or 'Getting colder' or 'Getting very hot!' as he gets closer to it.

As your baby gets older, he may even want to try hiding the toy himself! If so, do not find the toy too easily and when you do finally uncover it try to look surprised!

Key skills: Listening, memory and problem solving

30 The towers of power   *18 months–3 years*

For an older child there is nothing simpler than putting one thing on top of another but for a baby it is a real challenge and finding that things can fall down can be, at any age, a bit of a surprise! As your child gets more control of grasping and holding things introduce him to a range of stacking toys such as plastic cups or cones that can fit inside each other.

If it is too difficult at first begin with two at a time. See if he can put them together and pull them apart. Remember that each part of a stacking toy should be big enough for him to hold but not too small that it can be swallowed.

- **Stack it up**
  1 Give your child some stacking toys, showing how they fit together and stack up and saying what you are doing.
  2 Invite him to play with the stacking toys by putting two or more together.
  3 Talk to him as he plays, counting the toys being stacked and talking about the colour and size of each object. Offer a challenge from time to time such as 'Let's see how many we can put together . . .'

Trying to build things up is good for hand-eye coordination. Seeing when and why they fall is an early lesson in the logic of cause and effect. It also gives him a sense of choice and power.

- **The tower of power**
  For this you will need some building blocks or stacking toys or try stacking things and building towers with other things that come to hand, for example stones on a beach. You can also pile things up in a push-along toy or use packets from the kitchen.

  1 Show your baby how to make a tower out of building blocks or other stackable objects.
  2 Tell him you are going to knock it down and slowly push it over.
  3 Help him to build a tower then show him he has the power to push it over.

  Count the number of blocks and talk about size and describe how it comes crashing down!

Key skills: Physical skills, planning, problem solving, cause and effect, language and number.

2

Brain Games for young children (3–6 years)

The brain works best when the body is fit and healthy. A young child needs a rich diet of physical experience to help promote the growth of branches of the billions of brain cells that make up his brain. By creating a variety of activities for your child – dancing, rolling, crawling, turning, balancing, climbing, stretching, jumping, catching and so on it will not only be gym for the body but also the brain. Every day needs to be an exercise day – and a thinking day.

Remember that the child's growing brain needs six things to function well – supplies of good food, drink, oxygen (fresh air), physical exercise, rest and stimulus. They need both physical activity (such as *Brain gym* and *Balancing act* below) and mental stimulus (*mind gym*) that the following brain games will provide.

Children love routine, playing games they enjoy again and again, but they will also enjoy playing something new. Learning to think requires plenty of practice and variety, within a routine that makes them feel safe. Remember there is no one right way to play a game. So sometimes vary the games by adapting them and playing them in a different way. What is important is to give your child the mental stimulus they need for their intelligence to fully develop.

At the toddler stage children tend to be full of enthusiasm for new activities, and their growing ability to concentrate and follow complex directions make them a joy to play games or make things with. They learn best through play, and every activity listed here not only develops his thinking and physical skills but also gives you the chance to have lots of fun together.

From about the age of three children's brain development means they can begin creating their own personal stories with beginnings and endings using a growing range of words. Do not be afraid to use long words with children, they will probably enjoy the strange sound and want to enter into the adult world of long words from time to time. Try to use interesting and descriptive adjectives when you tell a story eg 'the wrinkled old lady trembled like leaf as the muffled sound of footsteps came closer and closer . . .'

Your young child will need to play with others, perhaps at a nursery or play group, as well as being introduced to a rich range of games at home. Regular play with other children and adults will also help your child enhance their language and thinking skills. A variety of games will help give your young child with the mental stimulus they need for their intelligence to fully develop (Games 31–60).

Fig 3

Brain Games for young children 3–6 years

31 Brain gym   *2 years and on*

Brain gym can be any game that presents a physical challenge, needs thinking about and is fun to play, for example playing with balls, running round obstacles, climbing up, learning a dance or a skipping rhyme, playing hopscotch, walking backwards, doing somersaults or standing on one's head! Brain gym includes any game that needs physical and mental effort, such as:

- **Ball games**
  Start off playing with a big beach ball, Then try playing with smaller balls – rubber balls, tennis balls, yarn balls, ping-pong balls and so on. Play simple versions of games like table tennis (hitting a ball to and fro), football (kicking a ball into a goal), cricket (throwing a ball at a target or hitting it with a bat), basket/netball (throwing a ball into a basket or bin) or bowling (rolling it to knock skittles down).

- **Catching games**
  Catching is quite a challenge for a young child. Begin with a soft ball. Tell him to look at the ball and get ready to catch it, then catch it. Encourage his attempts, for example by saying: 'You were really close' 'Hold your hands this way' or 'Keep watching the ball' Remember it is a skill that many grown-ups can fail at!

- **Bean bag games**
  Throwing odd objects such as bean bags can be fun from the age of three. Make some bean bags by pouring a cup of uncooked beans into a bag, seal it, put it into an old sock, seal and trim the edges. Play tossing the bags into a large bowl, at a target or into a circle drawn on the floor. See if he can walk balancing a beanbag on his head (see *Balancing Act* below)

- **Jumping games**

  Play 'jump the stream' by marking two parallel lines to represent a stream to be leapt over. When he succeeds increase the width to create more of a challenge. Measure and tell him how far he has jumped.

Play action games, for example by saying: 'Let's see how many jumps/hops/skips/spins can you do?' Talk about the shapes the body makes, the parts of the body and muscles used, count the number of times he can do things or measure the time taken (see also *Simon says* p37)

Key skills: Physical co-ordination, scientific, mathematical and language skills

32 Balancing act   *4 years on*

Experts say that complex physical activities involving the whole body, like crawling, swimming or balancing, help strengthen the pathways that link the two sides of the brain and improve the functioning of the brain. Take your child swimming and try some balancing games.

- **Balancing games**

  Invite your child to try balancing something on his head for example a book, a scarf, a feather, a pack of cards on his head and then move from one part of the house or garden to another. Challenge him, and others, to try walking along a straight line ('tightrope walking') with something balanced on their head. Have a race with a bean bag each on your head. Practice will help with both posture (standing/walking with body straight), muscle control and sense of balance.

Vary the game by inviting him to lay on his back and with feet in the air and balancing different items on the soles of his feet. When outside try balancing long thin items such as brooms or bats on his hands. Remember to make sure what he tries is safe.

- **Helicopter spin**
  Ask your child to stand with hands outstretched and spin round as fast as possible for 15 seconds. Say: 'Stop, close your eyes, keep your balance and stay standing.' Stand still for 30 seconds until he no longer feels dizzy. Try this up to ten times, one way only. Help by holding his hand to spin him if needed.

Older children can try *juggling* with two balls or bean bags, another complex physical skill good for stimulating both sides of the brain.

Key skills: Physical co-ordination, self control, balance and language skills

33 Question Games   *3 years and on*

Young children are full of questions that you may not always have time to answer. When you have the time encourage your child's natural curiosity about the world by him questions and inviting him to think for himself.

- **What do you think?**
  The questions to ask when your child is learning to speak are naming questions such as: 'What is this?' 'Who is this?' 'Where is . . . ?' From the age of about three begin asking 'Why?' questions. By asking 'Why?' questions you are

teaching him not just to accept everything but to find out how things work and why people do things. If he asks a question don't always give him an answer, play the game of saying: 'What do you think?' and encourage him to try to work out things for himself.

- **What am I thinking?**
  Think about something both you and your child know about, for example your pet, your car, or the clock on your wall. Start by saying: 'I am thinking of something. Try to find out what I am thinking of by asking me questions. You win the game if you can find out or guess what it is.' If your child finds this hard help him by giving clues, such as; 'It is something in this room' or 'What question would you ask to find out if it was a person?'

When he asks an interesting question, praise it by saying: 'That was a good question' – even if it has nothing to do with the topic in hand! And sometimes play the questions game by asking him one back: 'What do you think?'

Key skills: Questioning, language and reasoning about cause and effect.

34 Listen!   *3 years and on*

Children need to learn how to listen carefully and concentrate on things. Help your child to develop listening skills and concentration by playing listening games at home or when out for a walk.

- **Hunt-the-clock**
  (see p46)

- 'Hunt-the-thimble'
  Play using a thimble or any other small object, by whispering directions to your child, such as 'Walk into the garden. Take three steps left. Three steps forward. You are getting warmer . . . etc' Try reversing the game so your child hides the object and gives you the instructions to do the hunting.

- Blindfold games
  Sit him in a chair with eyes closed or blindfolded. Move about and make a sound, saying the initial of his name softly. He has to point to where the sound comes from. Get him to identify sounds you make like closing a door, rustling newspaper or pulling the curtains (for more blindfold games see p166)

- Sound-hunting
  Play 'What is that sound?' games when you out for a walk together. See if he can hear the wind rustling the leaves, a bird song or distant engine noise. Get him to close eyes to concentrate. When you get home see how many of the sounds he can remember.

Try whispering very quietly in his ear – can he still hear what you are saying?

Key skills: Questioning, reasoning and visual memory skills.

35 Pairs   *2–5 years*

Children enjoy matching and sorting games. These games teach that things of the same kind can have different shapes, sizes and colours.

- **Matching**
  The simplest game is to ask your child to find and match two similar objects out of a mixed collection of objects such as toy animals, bricks, colours, shapes. Other things to be sorted into pairs include socks or shoes. Put a lot of odd socks into a bag and every couple of weeks have a good sort into pairs!

- **Find the pairs**
  Card games are good for matching and sorting from about the age of three.
  Begin with *Find the pairs*. Sort out 5 pairs of cards (different numbers from same suits of two packs) and lay down one of each pair. Ask him to find and lay down the pairs from the remaining 5 cards. He does not need to count the number of symbols on the cards but match the cards visually. Later he will learn to count the numbers and play *Pairs* with a pack of cards (see p56)

- **Picture card snap**
  A fun first proper card game that is best played with two separate piles of cards. Different kinds of picture snap cards can be bought and then move on from these to using playing cards (see p74)

Key skills: Questioning, thinking things through, reasoning about cause and effect.

36 How many ways?   *4 years–adult*

I was reading my children the story of *Winnie the Pooh*, which begins: 'Here is Edward Bear, coming downstairs now, bump, bump, bump, on the back of his head, behind Christopher Robin. It is as far as he knows, the only way of coming downstairs, but sometimes he feels that there really is another way, if only he could stop bumping for a moment and think of it. And then he feels that perhaps there isn't . . .' I asked them if they could help Edward Bear (alias the Pooh) think of other ways to go downstairs.

Soon ideas began to flow: 'He could ask someone to carry him.' 'Why would they want to do that?' 'Well he could say to them 'If you carry me downstairs I'll tell you a funny joke"

'He could slide down the banister, holding his arms out like this to keep his balance', 'He could make a parachute out of a bedsheet and float down', 'He could sit on a tray like a sledge, and if it was the right angle slide down', 'They could fix a chair like a lift to the side of the stairs. He could sit in it and someone could pull him up and down', 'They could build a trapdoor and he could slide down a rope', 'If he did that mightn't he land on someone's head?' 'Not if the rope was tied to a bell, and every time he used it a bell rang.'

After we had finished thinking of ideas I asked how many different ways there were of coming down stairs and got the answer; 'No one knows, because someone might always think of another idea.' Whatever we are doing there may be other ways to do it. Have fun exploring these ways with your child.

- **How many ways?**
  Challenge your child to think of as many different ways to do an action as you can, for example: 'How many ways can you think of to cross the road?' Story books can provide good starting points for this game. Try asking: 'What other ways could the character do this?' make it a game by taking turns to think of different ways and stop when there is only one person left giving ideas – or when everyone is bored.

- **How many uses?**
  Take an everyday object, such as a plastic plate and ask 'What could this be used for?' (for example as a sunshade/hat, frisbee, a circle drawing, face mask, spinning on a stick, cover for something etc.) Praise your child for any interesting or fantastical suggestions he makes. How many uses can you

think of for a box, a towel, a nail, a brick, a sheet of paper, a plastic cup or an old sock?

Key skills: Develops language skills, creativity and imagination

37 Who's hiding there?' 3–5 years

A good memory game for a young child is 'Who is hiding there?' Play with any kind of picture cards or make your own using favourite characters or animals. Draw them or cut them from comics or magazines and stick them on card. Write the name of the picture on each card.

- **Who is hiding there?**
  1 Lay all the pictures cards down for your child to see.
  2 Slowly turn each picture face down.
  3 Point to a card and ask him 'Who is hiding here?' and wait for him to guess the picture on the turned-over card.
  4 Add challenge to the game by increasing the number of cards and then by moving the turned over cards to new positions, at first slowly one at a time.
  5 Later try moving the cards more quickly, and then moving two at a time, using both hands, to make the game even more challenging.

He will rely on memory of the pictures to start with, but if you use picture and word cards he will also try to remember them by recognising the names of the words. Let him play the game by testing you. Remember to praise him when he correctly identifies the hidden pictures.

Key skills: Develops memory, language and word recognition skills

38 What is it?   *3–6 years*

Guessing games are good for your child if they get him to think, puzzle things out and predict what the right answer might be. This game involves a mystery picture which you only show a bit of and he has to figure out what it is.

- **What is it?**
  Find some pictures of things your child knows in magazines. Cut out the pictures and paste them onto a separate piece of paper. Hide each picture in an envelope.
  1 Play the game by pulling the first picture out of the envelope just far enough for the child to see the bottom of the picture and ask: 'What is it?'
  2 Give clues, for example: 'What do you see? Two wheels? What might that be . . . a dog?'
  3 Pull the picture a little farther out so that new clues appear.
  4 Continue the game until he guesses what the picture is.

You can also play this game with picture books, by hiding most of the picture with a piece of paper and asking if your child to guess what the picture is.

Key skills: Develops perceptual, prediction and language skills

39 Letter games   *2 years on*

Have fun introducing your child to letters, by playing letter games, such as:

- **Tracing in the air**
  Trace letters in the air with your finger, for example your child's name: 'Let's make some big D's for Danny, and I'll hold your hand while we do it.'

- **Alphabet cookies**
  Make some alphabet cookies together. Use any biscuit recipe from a cook book. Make a lot of small cookies and use them to spell out the letters of your child's name or use the dough to make alphabet letters that spell his name.

- **Alphabet cards**
  Make a game from alphabet cards, for example pick an alphabet card from a pile and think of a word beginning with that letter.

- **Alphabet song**
  Teach your child an alphabet song – vary the way you sing, for example high, low, loud, softly, fast, slow, for each letter.

- **Alphabet bingo**
  Make bingo cards from card or blank postcards. Divide the card into 6 squares and print 6 different letters on each card. Cut up card into 5cm squares and write a letter on each square card. Play bingo in the usual way:
  1 Pull a letter from a bag or box and say eg 'B is for ball'.
  2 If your child has a 'b' on his card he covers it with a marker.
  3 The first to cover all six letters on their card is the winner.
  Play the game in two ways – with lower case and a new game with capital letters. Older children can run the game and say a word or make up a funny sentence for each letter.

- **Mystery letters**
  Stick a sheet of sandpaper onto card. Use this to cut out the letters of the alphabet. Cover a letter with cloth and see if your child can identify what letter it is by feel.

Trace letters on the back of his hand with your finger – can he say what letter it is? Trace letters in the air with him. When going round a supermarket see how many things your child can name beginning with different letters of the alphabet.

Key skills: Develops memory, letter recognition and language skills

40 I Spy   *3 years on*

Once your child knows about letters and letter sounds they can play that great game 'I-Spy' and some of its easier or harder variations, for example:

- **I Spy** Choose something that your child can see, for example a ball, and say 'I spy with my little eye something beginning with . . . B (or 'buh')' and see if your child can guess what it is.

- **Letter-spy** Ask him to collect in a bag or box any object beginning with a certain letter.

- **Made from-spy** Say 'I spy something made from . . . (a material eg wood/plastic/metal)

- **Shape-spy** Say 'I spy something that is a (eg round, oval, square) shape'

- **Purpose-spy** Say 'I spy something that we . . . (eg eat, drink, wear, use as a tool)

- **Rhyming-spy** Say 'I spy something that rhymes with . . .'

- **Picture book I-spy** Show an interesting picture from a book and say 'I spy with my little eye . . . (and give a clue, like 'something round')

- **Car I-spy** When on a car trip together say: 'Let's see who is the first to see something beginning with . . .' (for more car games see p177–181)

With older children move on to double letter sounds: 'I spy something beginning with . . . ch, dr, cl, br etc.' Later play the game using endings such as 'ed, ing, ay or ox'

Key skills: Develops memory and language (letter/sound perception and vocabulary skills)

41 Rhyming games   *3–6 years*

Rhyming games are excellent for developing language and phonic skills as well as helping your child develop their vocabulary. Reading a book of nursery rhymes can be turned into a game by simply inviting your child to add the rhyming word at the end of each verse.

- **Rhyming sounds**
  Start by saying a rhyming sound such as 'doo'. Your child must make a sound that rhymes with it, such as 'moo'. Take turns and see how many rhyming sounds you each can make. Start with simple sounds such as 'me', 'in' or 'say'. 'Say' for example rhymes with 'day, say, play, stay, way, hay, may, pay' and so on.

- **Rhyming riddles**
  Say a noun and your child must find a rhyme for it that makes sense, for example 'a bad . . . (dad)', 'a wet . . . (pet)', 'a bee in a . . . (tree)', 'a fish in a (dish)', 'a cat on a . . . (mat/hat/rat)' and so on.

- **Rhyming colours**
  Think of a colour and an object that rhymes with it eg a blue . . . (shoe), 'a red . . .(head), a black . . . (mac), 'a grey . . .(tray)' and so on

- **Make a rhyme**

  As your child grows older you will be able to create some rhymed verses together, where an adult says the first line and the child responds by adding a rhyming line as in this example: 'One two . . . a bird flew.' 'Three four . . . out the door.' 'Five six . . . Into some sticks.' 'Seven eight . . . and lay down straight.' 'Nine ten . . . on a big fat hen.' *Make a rhyme* can be played at any odd moment to add interest to any short sentence or saying.

Challenge you child to find a rhyme for any word you see or say. See also *Rhyming Tennis* p103.

Key skills: Develops memory, language (letter/sound recognition and phonic skills).

42 Musical jars   *3–6 years*

Young children enjoy the sound that tapping a spoon on a jar of water can make, even more if you have many jars that make different sounds. Help develop his musical and listening skills by playing *musical jars*.

- **Musical jars**
  1 Find 10 or 12 identical glass bottles or jars, a selection of different 'drumsticks' such as wooden and metal spoons, and a jug of water.
  2 With your child experiment in filling the jars with different amounts of water and seeing what sound they make when struck with different 'drumsticks'.
  3 Encourage your child to listen carefully to the fine differences in pitch made by striking jars containing different levels of water and to make his own 'water music'.

4 Add drops of different food colourings to the water in each
jar to add to the pleasure of playing your musical jars and
recognizing different musical notes.

Key skills: Developing musical and auditory discrimination.

43 Statues   *4–6 years*

Many games help develop physical control and mind/body co-
ordination, such as:

- **Statues**
  This game is a good way to quieten a group of noisy children.
  1 They start off by moving, walking or dancing around.
  2 When you give the word, such as 'Stop!' they must stay
    absolutely still in whatever position they are in at that
    moment.
  3 They can only move when you give the word, such as 'Go'.
    If they move after you say 'stop' they are out and have to sit
    down.
  4 Continue until there are only one or two children left.
  Suddenly freezing demands self control and a rapid response.
  Standing still is quite a physical challenge for most children,
  so praise those who can.

- **Tag**
  An energetic and popular variation of the *Statues* game.
  1 One child is 'on' and must try to catch and touch each of
    the others.
  2 When touched each child must freeze, like a statue, until
    brought alive by another child's touch.
  3 Change the child who is 'on' frequently and try to make
    sure all are given a turn.

- **Sleeping pirate**
  1 You play being a sleeping pirate sitting with your back to your child, or group of children, guarding a 'treasure' (which could be a sweet).
  2 Starting from the far side of the room each child tiptoes forward, trying to get nearer to the treasure.
  3 If you hear a sound you turn quickly round and open your eyes.
  4 If a child is frozen still like a statue he becomes invisible, waits until you turn back to 'sleep' then can carry on again. If you see a child moving they must go back to the start.
  5 The child who reaches you without being seen moving wins the game (or treasure). Children then can take turns being the sleeping pirate.

Key skills: Muscular control, physical co-ordination, self awareness, co-operation with others.

44 In my suitcase . . .   *4–6+years*

This popular family game has a number of variations.

- **Suitcase**
  1 Each person takes a turn to say: 'In my suitcase I packed a . . .' then names an object, such as 'towel'.
  2 The next person has to say 'In my suitcase I packed a towel and a . . .' (then names another object).
  3 Each player has to remember and say the whole list of objects before adding another. A player who cannot remember the list drops out.
  Note: You can choose to pack fantastic or surreal objects if you wish, like the Eiffel Tower.

- **Letter suitcase**
  In this version each object to be packed must begin with the same letter of the alphabet, for example the letter 'B' – 'biscuit', 'banana', 'baboon' and so on.

- **Alphabetical suitcase**
  In this game each object to be packed must begin with the next letter of the alphabet, for example 'apple', 'ball', 'crown' and so on.

- **My grandmother's cat**
  This is a game of adjectives (describing words).
  1 The first player says: 'My grandmother's cat is a . . . happy cat'.
  2 Others must think up other adjectives such as 'horrible', 'hungry', 'hopeless'.
  3 The simple game is for each player to say one adjective, in the harder version each player must remember the list of adjectives that others have used, for example 'furry, funny, fantastic.'
  4 Try using two words that start with the same letter, for example: 'My grandmother's cat loves sizzling sausages'.

When playing with adjectives beginning with 'f' someone said 'philosophical' We were not sure this was an 'f word' so we took a vote to see if 'f' sounding words should be allowed (the verdict was they should be). If in doubt about a word or rule have a vote.

These are good car games or to play at a party. Create your own variation, for example 'I went to the supermarket and I bought . . .' or take turns to suggest new starter words.

Key skills: Memory, vocabulary and language skills.

45 Naming games   *4–6+ years*

Naming games, like *Categories*, can be played anywhere to provide fun and stimulate thinking. Thinking in categories is one of the most important of human thinking skills.

- **'How many can you name?'**
  Simply choose a category and challenge family members to name as many items as they can that fit in that category, for example: zoo animals, kinds of clothes, things to drink, things with wheels, things that float, things that fly, items of furniture, vegetables, fruit, things in the kitchen, things made of wood, musical instruments, countries, types of sport and so on.

- **Alphabetical names**
  Each person must say a word that fits into a given category, for example boys' names, girls' names, or items in supermarket – using the next letter of the alphabet. If letters are too hard, such as 'x' and 'z' just leave them out.

- **How many words?**
  Take turns to think of words to describe, for example:
  A person (happy, tall, small, ugly, famous, sad, angry, scared, surprised, sleepy etc.)
  A building (old, modern, ugly, brick, wooden, tall, ruin, castle, skyscraper etc.)
  Food (salty, tasty, sweet, hot, frozen, sticky, creamy, baked, boiled, roasted etc.)
  Music (loud, soft, beautiful, slow, pop, classical, folk, hip-hop etc)
  The way animals move (hop, scamper, slithis, creep, leap, race, sprint, pace etc.)

Older children can think of more difficult categories such as words for metals, weather, cold-blooded animals or things that are hard, soft, smooth, sticky. Think of words to describe a summer day, a winter day, a dark night, getting caught in the rain, fireworks, a birthday party etc.

Key skills: Memory, vocabulary and language skills.

46 Tossing games   *3–6+ years*

For this game you will need a good supply of buttons, counters, coins, acorns or other small objects (anywhere between five and twenty) and a box, basket or bin to throw them in. You will also need a ruler or line on the floor to stand behind. The aim is to improve your child's skill in throwing and to practice counting by keeping the score.

- **The tossing game**
  1 Give your child a number of buttons (or whatever objects you have). Say: 'Stand behind the line. Throw one button at a time. See how many you can get into the bin.'
  2 When all the buttons have been thrown count the number in the bin. That is the score. Now try again with more buttons or use the same buttons as before.
  3 Take turns and add the number each player gets in the bin to their score. Keep counting as the game progresses.
  The success of your child in tossing buttons into a bin will improve with practice. And practicing means counting to find out 'how many' over and over again.
    Create your own tossing games, for example pebbles into a circle of sand on the beach, peas into a bucket, hoops over stick etc. Older children will enjoy other target games involving adding the score up, for example:

- **Into the eggbox**
  Tear the top off an old eggbox. Put a different number in each section of the egg carton (if it had 6 eggs, put one number in each section ie 1, 2, 3, 4, 5, 6) Give your child a number of small things to toss like beads, beans, paper clips, buttons, peas, marbles. When an object lands into the carton it scores the number given to that section. Older children may prefer to play tiddlywinks, which involves trying to make plastic counters jump into the numbered sections of an eggbox.

- **Card toss**
  A pack of playing cards are dealt out to the players who then take turns tossing their cards onto the floor. If a player tosses card that lands on another they pick both up. The player who picks up most or all the cards is the winner.

Key skills: Physical co-ordination, throwing and counting skills.

47 Story telling games   *4–6+ years*

Every story is a kind of game with words. To be able to create good stories of his own your child needs to hear many other stories and you can be his most important storyteller. The more stories you share with your child the better he will get at making up his own stories. The age of four is a good time to encourage story telling and story writing. However, don't forget, you can start reading and telling stories to your child from 3 months onwards.

Here are some story games to play:

- **The story telling game**
  1 Choose a character your child knows or one you make up.
    Four year olds often like to have a story about someone

with their own name. But it could also be about an animal or a monster.

2 Begin the story and then stop and ask your child to carry on.

3 When your child stops you carry on and the story continues by turns until it ends or your child is fed up with it.

If the story went well try later to remember what happened in the story with your child.

- **Story writing**

  Start your child off telling a story as above. This time use some plain sheets of paper and write the story as it is being told. If your child struggles with making up a story get him to tell a story he already knows. Can he make up a different ending? What happens after the story ends? When the story is finished staple the pages together and encourage your child to illustrate the story.

- **Stories about special times**

  Make up a story or story book with your child about special times, like birthdays, parties or holidays. Try and add photos or pictures to your story. Bring it out regularly for him to read with you.

- **Story lines**

  Story lines tests your child's abilities to re-construct a story they know well.

  1 Choose a story with about 7 characters, from your child's favourite book. Draw, trace, or cut out pictures from a duplicate of your child's story book. Paste each character onto a separate pieces of paper.

  2 Say 'Who is this?' and see if they can name and tell you about each character.

  3 See if they can retell the story using their own words with these simple visual reminders.

Later they will be able to draw upon their experience of hearing and playing with stories to create their own stories, either about their own adventures or fantasy stories about magic, princes and princesses, ghosts and strange happenings.

See 'Story chain' p108.

Key skills: Language and creative thinking skills.

48 Making mixtures   *4–6+ years*

Start teaching your child how to cook by allowing him making his own mixtures. Through cooking, making mixtures and helping in the kitchen children can learn a lot about basic mathematics and science and also develop their reading skills.

- **Making mixtures**
  1 Begin by making play dough together (see p28). Encourage your child to make their own dough by adding ingredients such as food colouring or dried fruits.
  2 Try making smoothies and home made milkshakes. Show how to mix milk, ice cream or yoghurt and various fruits in a blender. Invite your child to taste the mixture and to experiment with different fruit variations.
  Most new ideas are combinations of old elements and food mixtures are great for proving the point. It will also give your child the confidence to use recipes in making mixtures.

- **Cook it!**
  1 Write out favourite recipes for your four year olds in bold printing.
  2 Then encourage your child to prepare the recipe. Make it a game not a serious 'you must do this, you must do that' kind of test.

3 Follow the written recipe but be prepared for your child to experiment as they go along or think of a new idea (unless of course his ideas are clearly unhygienic or positively poisonous!) Make the recipes you write together a reason to read.

When cooking talk about ingredients and the reason for each step, such as how eggs, milk and flour combine together. Every time you cook with your child challenge him to think about what he is mixing, how much he is mixing and what he might do with the results.

Key skills: Maths, science and language skills, creativity, confidence and ability in cooking.

49 What's missing? 4–6+ *years*

This is a problem solving game that develops observation skills and memory. You can make this very simple or quite hard depending on the age of your child.

- **What's missing?**
  1 Place five or more different objects (for example toys or kitchen utensils) on a tray and cover the objects with a piece of cloth.
  2 Remove the cloth and show the objects to your child.
  3 Ask your child to close his eyes (or turns his back) so he cannot see as you remove one item from the tray.
  4 When you are ready the child opens his eyes (or turns around) and tries to guess which object is missing.

At first start out with just a few objects and, and after your child has succeeded several times with this number, increase the challenge by adding more objects. Sometimes reverse the roles and let your child find some objects for you to guess which have been removed.

When you play this game again use different kinds of objects, for example: a group of toys, different coloured crayons, letters of the alphabet, pictures cut from magazines, playing cards, jigsaw pieces and so on. You can also play it around the house, by removing something that is usually there and saying for example: 'What is missing from the dining table/mantelpiece/garden?'

See also *Kim's Game* p99.

Key skills: Observation, concentration and memory skills.

50 Snap!   *4–6+ yrs*

Snap is a great way to introduce your child to the pleasure of playing cards. It is a fast game that will help him to think quickly, to concentrate and to practice matching card numbers and symbols. The game is for two players and the aim is to collect all your opponents' cards.

- **Snap!**
  1 Shuffle a standard pack of 52 cards.
  2 Deal out all the cards between two players (or if you want to be quick simply cut the pack into two roughly equal piles – giving your child the slightly larger pile).
  3 Each player either holds their cards in a pile in the hand or leaves the pile in front of them. There are two versions of this game:

Version 1: The game begins when each player turns their top card over *at the same time* and places it face up in front of them. If the cards are a matching pair the players shout *Snap!* The first person who says this collects their opponent's cards and adds them to the bottom of his pile. Young players may struggle with the idea of turning two cards over at the same time. If that happens try:

Version 2: Players simply play their cards alternately onto a central pile and shout *Snap!* when the card played matches the card on the top of the pile. The first person to shout 'Snap!' picks up all the cards.

Snap can be played with three or more players. The rules are the same but for this you will need two packs of properly shuffled cards. You can also play with packs of picture cards, but by using a 52 card pack your child will learn the value of each card, as well as the symbols and suits.

When children play together the winner is the one who wins all the 52 cards, and the loser is often the child complaining loudly of being cheated! When played well the game is good for developing a sense of fair play and coping with frustration and loss.

Another good card game for young children is *Old Maid*.

Key skills: Quick thinking, memory, concentration and card matching skills.

51 Pairs   *3–6+ years*

The aim of Pairs is to locate matching pairs of playing cards and collect more of them than other players. It can be played with two or more players.

- **Pairs**
  1 Shuffle the cards and lay the cards out (as in fig below) *face*

down on a flat surface and spaced out in four long rows of
13 cards each.

2 The youngest child begins by turning over two cards from
the layout.

3 If the two cards are of equal value (say two of hearts and
two of clubs or two kings) the player keeps them, and turns
over two more cards.

4 If the cards do not match the cards are returned face down
and the next player has a turn.

5 The players take turns until there are no cards left to play.
The player who has collected most cards is the winner.

Tip: Make sure that during play the layout of cards does not get
too messed up or that cards start overlapping.

Pairs is a great game for testing your child's ability to mem-
orize the positions of the cards as they are turned over then
turned face down. If older children find this game too easy make
the game colour specific, so that the pairs have to be either red
or black (so if the two of hearts is turned over the only matching card will be the two of diamonds).

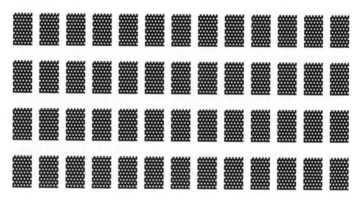

Fig 4 Card layout for the game

Key skills: Memory, concentration and number recognition skills.

52 Drawing games   *5–10 years*

Encourage your child to develop drawing and visual thinking skills by making drawings, such as portraits of his family or simple maps of his room. Here are some more simple drawing games:

- **Funny folk**
  1 Each player has a piece of paper and draws the top half of a funny person, animal or monster, without showing it to other players.
  2 When players have finished they fold the paper over so only the bottom of the picture can be seen.
  3 Players swap their folded drawings with each other, then complete their given picture by drawing the bottom half of the funny person, animal or monster.
  4 When the hidden drawings are finished players unfold and reveal their drawings.

- **Dotty drawings**
  This is a simple game is fun and challenging enough for younger and older children. It only needs pencil and paper. Any number can play.
  1 Each player draws six random dots on their page.
  2 The pages are shuffled and handed round.
  3 Players use the dots to draw a picture of anything at all, such as an animal, a funny face or scene. Give players up to three minutes to finish their picture.
  4 Players then show their drawing to everyone else. The game shows that everyone can draw and think creatively, though some may be better than others!
  Instead of dots, each player can draw three random lines (straight or curved) or shapes for another player to complete. See also Squiggles (p122).

- **Boxes**

  Boxes is a simple pencil and paper strategy game.

  1 Draw a grid of ten equally spaced dots on a sheet of paper, and then repeat the pattern downwards until there are ten rows of ten dots (as in fig 5). Younger children may prefer a smaller grid of six rows of six dots.

  2 Players take it in turns to draw a straight line (horizontal or vertical, but not diagonal) between two adjacent boxes.

  3 Each player tries to complete a small square by drawing the fourth line around it. A player who completes a square puts his initial in it and can draw another line.

  The winner is the player who has more squares completed at the end of the game. Thinking is needed to draw lines that make squares or will stop your opponents completing squares.

  Encourage your child to draw the grid for the next game.

- **Worm**

  Worm uses the same 10 × 10 grid as Boxes (see fig 5 below).

  1 One player draws a straight line (either vertical or horizontal, but not diagonal) between any two adjacent dots on the grid and draws a small circle on one end of the line to mark the worm's head.

  2 The next player then joins the other end of the line (the tail) to another adjacent dot.

  3 Players take it in turns to continue drawing lines from the tail to any dot next to it, with the aim of forcing the other player into a position where they cannot draw a line to any other nearby, vacant dot.

  4 The winner is the last player to draw a valid line extending the tail.

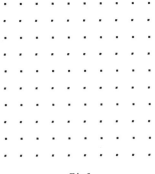

Fig 5

Key skills: Creative, visual and drawing skills.

53 Deduction games   *4–6+ years*

A deduction is when use a logical reason or series of reasons to solve a puzzle or problem. Games of deduction can be played at any time. Tell your child he is being a detective trying to solve a mystery from clues that are given.

- **Deduction**
  The game requires you to make up some simple clues. Your child must try to make a deduction from the two or more separate pieces of information you give them, for example:
  'I am holding something to my ear and talking. What am I doing?' (Using my mobile/ telephone)
  'I am holding a rod in my hand and am standing in water. What am I doing?' (Fishing)
  'I am watching monkeys in a cage and hearing lions roar. Where am I?' (At the zoo)
  'I have bought a ticket and am standing on a platform. Where am I?' (At a railway station)

'I can see daffodil flowers in the garden. What time of year is it?'

'I am eating a bowl of cereal and drinking orange juice. What time of day is it?'

'I am thinking of an animal that hops and croaks. What is it?'

'I am thinking of something wet, frozen and falls from the sky. What is it?'

Sometimes evidence may suggest more than one possible answer. Tell your child some a simple scenario and see if he can think of more than one possible reason for it. For example:

'I am wrapping up a present for someone. Why might I be doing that?'

'A little girl all alone, is crying in the street. Why might that be?'

'If you were walking on the grass and kicked something hard, what might it be?'

'How do you know if someone is hurt?'

When you are out together and see something strange ask him: 'Why is that there?' or 'What do you think is happening?' Encourage him to make up his own clues or take turns to ask the questions. Later try to add three or more bits of information, for example: 'Dan is taller than Jill. Jill is taller than Tom. Who is the tallest?'

Key skills: Logic, reasoning and language skills.

54 Number games   4– 6+ *years*

Whenever you play games using numbers you are helping to develop your child's number skills. The following games will help develop his number sense and help make him 'number friendly'.

- **Do it before I count to . . .**

  Whenever you have something you want your child to do make it into a game by suggesting they do it by the time you count to . . .(whatever number seems best), for example:

  'Wash your hands before I count to 20'

  'Finish your supper before I count in tens to 200'

  'Get dressed before I count in fives up to 100'

  'Towel yourself dry before I count backwards from 20 to 1'

  Try each time to vary your way of counting, for example by twos, threes, fours, fives, tens, hundreds, in halves, quarters and backwards so it remains a game.

  If you have no special jobs you want your child to do ask him to do some silly things like:

  'Tiptoe across the room before I count to . . .

  'Walk backwards to the end of the garden and back before I count to . . .'

  'Hop upstairs to bed before I count to . . .'

  You will be surprised how a game like this will help your child to count up to large numbers or to begin learning the basics of multiplication.

- **Join the numbers**

  This simple pen and paper game that is suitable for younger and older children. It can help children to learn and recognise written numbers.

  1 One player writes the numbers 1 to 21 at random all over a sheet of paper. The other player then also writes the numbers 1 to 21 at random on the same paper, making sure that any number is not too close to its identical number.

  2 The first player draws a line (straight or curved) to join two of the same number (for example, the two 4s). The next player then draws a line between any other identical

numbers (for example, the two 13s), making sure the line does not cross the line already drawn.

3 Players take it in turns to draw lines (without crossing other lines) until one player cannot link any identical numbers. The last player to join a pair of numbers wins.

It takes strategic thinking to plan your earlier lines to make sure your opponent cannot place the last line in the game.

Key skills: Number, thinking and drawing skills

55 Can you remember?   *3–6+ yrs*

Like other powers of the mind your child's memory can be trained. Challenge him to remember things from earlier in the day, ask him what happened yesterday, last week, last month, last year and so on. At bedtime ask him to recall his day, the story he read, what he saw or a conversation he had. Maybe mum, or one partner, does this one night and dad or the other partner the next. Encourage him to make 'mental pictures' in his head to help him remember. Ask him to remember an interesting sight you saw together. How many things that he saw can he remember? Does he remember something you don't? Do you remember anything that he doesn't?

- **Picture memory game**
  Choose an interesting picture from a favourite picture book. Ask him to study the picture carefully because you are going to play a memory game. Turn the page, or close the book, and see how many different things he can remember from the picture. Can he remember ten things?

  You can also play the memory picture game after you have been to a gallery or seen any interesting picture. A variation is to ask your child to draw what he remembers and then compare his drawing to the original picture.

For more memory games to play with older children see *Memory games* p99 and *Pelmanism* p144.

Key skills: Memory, vocabulary and language skills.

56 Silly me! *3–6 years*

Young children love silly jokes and word play. If they hear you playing 'Silly me' games they will soon start making up their own creative word combinations. Being silly can be fun.

- **Silly me!**
  1 For 'Silly me' you make up a nonsense sentence, for example: 'For dinner today I had fish with hats on'.
  2 You then invite a response, for example: 'What did you have for dinner today?' You hope he will reply with an equally silly sentence, such as 'For dinner today I had eggs with boots on'.
  3 If he does not reply, or after he has replied, you say another silly sentence, for example; 'For tea tonight I am having teddies on toast', and so on.

- **The cat and bear game**
  This silly word and observation game for 3–4 year olds can be played anywhere.
  1 You say 'Find me a . . . (then name something he can spot, for example 'a red car') Mr. Cat'
  2 When he spots it he replies 'Look over there Mr. Bear.'
  3 You reply 'I can see that Mr. Cat.'
  Look towards the object as you name it to make it easier to find. If he finds saying the words hard at first just ask him to point.

Key skills: Language, creative thinking and social skills (turn-taking)

57 Tick tack toe games   *4 years–adult*

Tick tack toe, or *noughts and crosses* is a simple pencil and paper game for two players. To win the game calls for luck if it is played without thinking or strategic thinking if you want to win. It is played on a 3x 3 grid (see fig 6) drawn on paper. It can be played by drawing the noughts and crosses or by using 3 counters each (or other pieces) to play with.

- **Tick tack toe or Noughts and crosses**
  Players take turns marking the spaces in a 3×3 grid with either an O or an X. The player who succeeds in placing three Os or Xs in a horizontal, vertical, or diagonal row wins the game.
  1 Decide which player is to be O and which is to be X. Usually X goes first.
  2 The first player places an x anywhere within the 9 boxes on the board.
  3 The next player places on O in any spare space.
  4 Players take turns until one player has three of his X or Os in a row (either horizontally, vertically or diagonally). If neither player succeeds it is a draw (which often happens).
  There is a winning strategy which means the first player to go cannot be beaten. Can you and your child discover what this strategy is? Try inventing, with your child, your own version of the game using different arrangements of squares or other shapes.

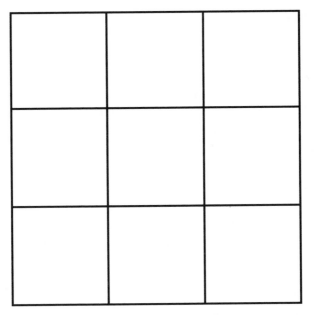

Fig 6 Tick tack toe or Noughts and Crosses

- **Avoid two (or three)**
  Avoid two is played on a chess or draughts (checkers) board with 8 draughts or counters each and the aim of the game is *not to get two of your counters in a row* either vertically, horizontally or diagonally.
  1 Players take turns to place their counters on the board.
  2 Check each time that neither player has two in a row.
  3 Continue playing until one player puts two in a row. He then *loses* the game.
  Avoid three is a more complex version of this game in which neither player must make a line of three, either vertically, horizontally or diagonally.
  See *Nine Men's Morris* p121.

Key skills: Strategic thinking, planning and problem solving.

58 Dice games   *4+ years*

Board games often use dice, for example in race games like
Snakes and Ladders. But many fun games can be played using
only dice. By the way, one 'dice' is called a die and the plural of
die is dice. You can make your own dice, for example with sugar
cubes – putting the numbers 6 and1, 5and 2, and 4 and 3 are
opposite each other.

- **Dice battle**
  The simplest game is for each player to throw a die and see
  who gets the highest score and either add the scores towards
  a target score of 50 or count the number of battles won (say
  up to 10).

- **Beat that!**
  Beat That! is a great game for teaching younger children the
  concept of place value. All you need is two dice and pencil and
  paper to keep the score. Older children can use more dice (up
  to seven dice) to make it more interesting. The aim is to get
  the highest score after a certain number of rounds.
  1 Each player throws all the dice. They then arrange them
    into the largest number using the values of the dice and
    say, "Beat . . .". For example, if a player threw a "3" and
    a "4", they would count that as 43 rather than 34 and
    would say, "Beat 43!". Their score is written on the score
    sheet.
  2 Each player takes it in turns to throw the dice, work out
    their highest score and say, 'Beat That!'
  3 Play continues for five rounds, with their score for each
    round added to their previous score.
  4 The player with the highest overall score at the end of the
    fifth round wins.

One variations is to make the aim to achieve the *smallest* total score possible. Older children who understand place value, can use up to seven dice to calculate their highest number up to millions! For example the if he throws 3, 1, 6, 2, 1, 4, 5 his best score would be 6, 543, 211

Key skills: Mathematical and numerical skills including understanding of place value

59 Hunting games   *3–6 years*

Children love the idea of hunting, hence the popularity of books like Michael Rosen's 'We're Going on a Bear Hunt'. The following are some hunting games that challenge them to solve problems and become hunters or detectives themselves.

- **Squirrel at the picnic**
  For this game you will need some picnic equipment such as blanket, basket, napkins, plates, bottle of water, food containers etc.
  1 Lay out a blanket and five things that you would take to a picnic – for example, a basket, napkins, plates, bottle of water, food container.
  2 Sit with your child on the blanket and show him all the items.
  3 Tell your child to close their eyes and take one item away.
  4 Once they open their eyes see if he/she can tell which item was taken by 'the squirrel who came to the picnic'! This game is fun for the whole family; older siblings love to be the squirrel!

- **Hunting for dinosaurs**
  This game can be played indoors or outdoors. You need one

large basket and a collection of toys such as plastic dinosaurs, stuffed animals or some other favourite set of toys.

1 Give your child a large basket and ask him to collect all of his chosen toys eg dinosaurs.

2 Once he has them all, count them according to size (e.g., 11 large, 8 medium and 7 small).

3 Then send him into another room, and stay there until called (older children can count up to 50 or 100, giving you enough time to hide the toys).

4 While the child is behind closed doors, hide all the dinosaurs around the house in plain view.

5 Once they are all hidden, give the child the basket and send him off on his dinosaur hunt.

6 When he thinks he has found them all, he has to count them again to be sure.

Key skills: Problem solving and creative thinking skills

60 Guessing games   *3–6 yrs*

In life we often have to manage with incomplete knowledge and so does your child. What we don't know we have to guess. Some guesses are better than others. Good guesses are ones we have a reason to make. If we use what we know as clues or have a reason for a particular guess it is called an 'educated guess'. If we don't think about it but guess randomly it is a 'wild guess'. Another word for 'educated guess' is hypothesis. Creating hypotheses is the first stage of scientific enquiry. Try to encourage your child not to make wild guesses but to hypothesise and use what he knows as clues, just like a scientist or detective.

- **Can you guess?**
  This game is a variation of '20 questions' (see p92) and can be played anywhere.
  1 Say to your child, 'I am thinking of something. Can you guess what this is? Here is a clue . . .'
  2 Start giving clues, one by one. For example, 'It is small,' 'It is furry', 'It has four feet' etc
  3 Encourage him to guess something. If it is not a correct guess, give him another clue. 'It drinks milk.' If he still does not guess it, keep giving clues. When he finally guesses, for example 'It's our kitten,' he will want to play again.
  Invite an older child to give you 'a hard one to guess.'

- **What's in the sock?**
  This activity helps children focus on their sense of touch.
  For this you will need a sock and small objects for the children to touch
  1 Place a small object inside a large tube sock.
  2 Ask your child to stick his hand inside the sock, feel the object, and try to guess what it is.
  Choose items such as a coin, button, stone, balloon, pencil or small toy.

When he makes a guess try asking: 'Why did you guess that?' and see if he has a reason. Was it an educated guess?

Key skills: Critical thinking (reasoning) and scientific (hypothesising) skills

3

Brain Games for your young junior (6–9 years)

Children need the stimulus of mental exercise to keep their minds in trim. Like a muscle the human mind expands and develops with use, and is kept fit through regular activity and exercise. It is something that children also want for themselves. As Sophie, aged 8, said 'I wish I had a bigger brain.' Sophie cannot change her brain but what she can do is make better use of it and brain games will help.

When he is 6 or 7 years old your child's brain will have a spurt of growth. He will learn and remember more easily and solve problems, his thinking will increase in speed, and he will remember more. He will begin to understand symbols like numbers and be able to play more challenging word and number games.

Children of 6–9 years often enjoy outdoor play with other children as well as indoor play. His physical abilities have improved and he will enjoy bicycle riding, sports activities, dancing, and other physically active play skills. Broaden your child's exposure to sports, dance, martial arts, and the like to use his new physical abilities and build his self confidence.

Playing on his own is also important, for example playing with action figures or dolls, organizing collections of toys or trading cards. This gives him time to think, and an escape from the fights and arguments that often break out in his peer group. He will also enjoy playing board and card games with others. Let him play the games he likes, but also introduce him to new brain games that challenge his thinking as well as providing fun times with the family (games 60–90).

Fig 7

Brain games for your young junior 6–9 years

61 Twenty Questions
62 Only joking!
63 Connect
64 Origami house
65 Would you rather?
66 Memory games
67 Jumbled up games
68 Who is it?
69 Rhyming tennis

61 Twenty Questions   *6–11+ years*

This is an old favourite, but can get people thinking hard at any age. The game can be played at any time and the rules are simple.

- **Twenty Questions**
  1 One person thinks of an object, then decides whether it is either:
    - *animal* (a live animal or is made from part of an animal like wool, leather or milk),

- *vegetable* (a plant or product that comes from plants such as wood, rubber) or
- *mineral* (anything else, such as metal, stone, plastic or other material)

or a combination of these

2 Players take turns to ask the person who thinks of an object questions to try to find out what the object is. The only answer that can be given is 'yes' or 'no'. If a player can guess the object before 20 questions are asked they win, if not then the person thinking of the object wins.

3 The person who wins thinks of the next mystery object, or turns are taken for this.

Start with simple things around the house. Show him how to discover the answer by a process of elimination, rather than by random guesses. For example if it is an animal good questions might be 'Is it bigger than a dog?' (finding the size), 'Is it a wild animal?' (to see what kind of animal), 'Does it have four legs? (helps exclude people, birds, fish and insects). A variation of Twenty Questions is *Who am I?*

- **Who am I?**
  In this game a player goes out of the room while the others decide what well known real or fictional character this person, for example a TV personality or story character (make sure it is a character the person will know). The player is then asked to return and has 20 questions to try and find out who he or she is.

Key skills: Logic, language, questioning skills and speed of thinking.

62 Only joking!   *6–11+ years*

What is your child's favourite joke? Here is the favourite joke of
a five year old:

Question: What did one grape say to the other grape?
Answer: Nothing, you silly. Grapes can't talk.

This ability of the brain to make connections is the source of
human learning, all of our creativity and culture. It is also the
reason we laugh at a joke or can solve a riddle. What makes us
laugh is the creative connection in a joke between two unex-
pected ideas. Brainpower is built by making connections and
telling jokes is an important aspect of the creative use of words.
So, whenever you can, share a joke with your child.

- **Crack a joke**
  Has anything funny happened to you today? Tell your child
  about it. Encourage them to share their funny moments with
  you. Share your child's interest in jokes, puns and riddles.
  Here is a joke recently told to me by a child:

  Child: Knock, knock.
  Me: Who's there?
  Child: Joe
  Me: Joe who?
  Child: No Joe King!

  Can you, or your child, make up any more 'Knock Knock'
  jokes?
      Swap jokes with your child. If you don't know any jokes
  that would appeal to children buy or borrow a joke book or
  find some on the net. Encourage your child to find jokes for
  you. When I asked a child for her favourite joke she replied:
  'Can you describe a hungry horse in four letters?' Me (after
  some thought) 'No'. Child:' MTGG (empty gee gee)!'.

- **Riddles**

  Riddles are a very old and universal king of word game. What riddles does your child know?

  The following riddle was the favourite of an eight year old: Question: What pets make the most noise? (Answer: Trumpets). Make up some riddles or buy a book of riddles for children.

See also Tongue twisters p129.

Key skills: Language and social skills.

63 Connect   *6–11+ years*

Making connections is the way a child creates an understanding of the world. Making new connections is the basic process of all creative thinking. This game challenges children to make creative connections between words. Most words express ideas about things, but some words don't, they simply connect other words together, for example 'and', 'because' and 'then'. The ideas that words express are called concepts. Some words or concepts are linked, but not all ideas have a direct link or connection. '*Connect*' is a kind of 'word tennis' game that challenges players to make creative connections between words.

- **Connect**
  1 Explain how one word has a connection in meaning with another, for example 'foot' connects with 'ball' because you can kick a ball with a foot. 'Foot' could also connect with toes, leg and with other words. The word 'tree' has a connection with 'leaf' or 'wood', but maybe not with 'kettle'.
  2 Say a word and see if your child can find a connecting word, for example 'hat'

3 You must then find a word that connects with your child's
   word, for example 'head'
4 Continue to take turns until one of you cannot think of a
   word or the last word spoken has no connection with the
   previous word. If players cannot see a connection they can
   challenge by saying 'What is the connection?'

Connect can be played with any number of players taking turns.
When there are more than two of you any disputes about whether
one word really connects with another can be decided by vote.
The way to avoid disputes is simply to start the game again.

- **What links them?**
  Say to your child 'I am thinking of two things, can you say
  what might link them (or can you see how they are connected?)' for example 'egg' and 'book'. (Birds lay eggs and you
  can read recipes using eggs in a book).

Ask your child: 'Can you think of two words that cannot be connected by an idea?' Related games to play with older children are
'Word links' (p135) and 'Disconnections' (see p153).

Key skills: Language skills, concept building and creative
thinking.

64 Origami house   *6–11+ year olds*

'Origami' is a Japanese word meaning paper folding. It is a skill
that Japanese are taught as children and still practice as adults.
It is both an art form and a practical means of learning how to
make models and beautiful wrappings. Young children will need
help so it is a good idea to practice it yourself before introducing
it to them. A fun way to begin is to make an origami house.

To make an origami house you will need to start with a plain A4 size sheet of white paper. In origami it is a good idea to have several sheets handy in case of mistakes!

- **Origami house**
  To make an origami house show your child how to fold the paper as follows:

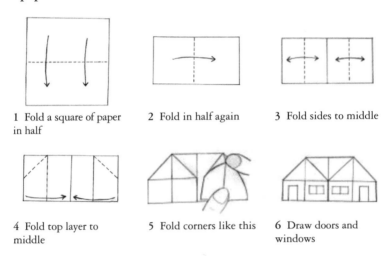

1 Fold a square of paper in half

2 Fold in half again

3 Fold sides to middle

4 Fold top layer to middle

5 Fold corners like this

6 Draw doors and windows

Fig 8 Stages in making an origami house

Once the 'house' is made it can be decorated with coloured pens or pencils and a surprise drawn on the inside.

Key skills: Manipulative dexterity, creativity and ability to follow instructions.

65 Would you rather? *6–11+ years*

Would you rather? is a simple question and answer game to challenge your child's thinking. You play by giving them a choice between two alternatives and asking 'Which would you prefer?'

or 'Would you rather?' The choice might be between any two objects, pictures, persons, places, feelings, words or imaginary things. A simple choice between one or another might be easy, but the follow-up adds challenge – 'Say *why*.' And '. . . and any other reasons?'

You can play the game any time and anywhere, perhaps taking a cue from what you are seeing or doing, for example reading a book or watching TV ask would you rather be . . . (this character) or . . . ? (another character).

Here are some examples of 'Would you rather . . . ?' questions to ask:

- **Would you rather?**
  Would you rather be a butterfly or a bee?
  Would you rather be a river or a bridge
  Would you rather be a child or an adult?
  Would you rather be rich or happy?
  Would you rather be an ant or an elephant?
  Would you rather be red or green?
  Would you rather be yes or no?
  Would you rather be a forest or a stream?
  Would you rather be rich or happy?
  Would you rather be a table or a chair?
  Would you rather live in the country or town?
  Would you rather have £50 or 5 friends?
  Would you rather go through a door to another world or have free sweets for the rest of your life? Why?

Develop the game by asking your child to choose between three or more alternatives, for example: *Would you rather live in a house surrounded by the sea, snow or the jungle? Why?* Older children can be given more open-ended choices for example, *Would you rather be a colour or a sound? Which colour or sound? Why?*

After the game ask children to think up different sorts of

dilemmas themselves. Examples from children include: Would you rather be a horse, a dog, a pig or a spider? Would you rather be a giant or a dwarf? Would you rather have a million pounds and be rich, or be poor and live forever? See also John Burningham's picture book called *Would You Rather?*

Key skills: Language, reasoning and creative thinking skills

66 Memory games   *7–11+ years*

A child's memory can improve through training and important memories are kept alive by repeated recall. Memory games can help improve your child's capacity to remember.

Kim's game first appeared in Rudyard Kipling's book 'Kim' and formed part of the hero's training. Kim had to sit cross-legged in front of a low table on which his teacher placed various stones, beads and other objects of different size, shape and colour. After a short while these were covered up and Kim was asked to recall all the objects and their positions on the tray. The more he practised the better at remembering he became. See if this is also true with your child.

'*Kim's game*' can be played with one or more children. You will need a tray, a cloth to cover it and an assortment of different objects.

- **Kim's game**
  Here are two versions of *Kim's game*:
  1 Place up to ten common objects on a tray. Show them to your child and tell him to try to remember what he can see. After one minute cover the tray, or hide it away. Then ask him to say, or write down, as many things as he can remember. If two or more children are playing the one who remembers most wins.

2 After seeing the objects on the tray either the child is sent
   out of the room, or blindfolded him so he cannot see. You
   then rearrange the objects, replacing some, then call him
   back (or remove the blindfold) and see if he can spot what
   has been moved.

Add more items to make the game more challenging. See also
The minister's cat p149.

- **Memory pictures**
  In this game it is pictures not objects that have to be remembered. Show your child ten pictures, hide them then ask how
  many he can remember. An added challenge is to number the
  pictures, then say, for example; 'Can you remember picture
  number 5?'
     Memory games can also be played with words or numbers,
  for example write ten random words or numbers on a piece of
  paper, show it to your child for one minute, cover it and see
  how many your child can remember. See also the memory
  game: *Pelmanism* p144.

Talk to your child about different ways of remembering things,
such as by initial letters (mnemonics), colours or by making up
a story that links several things to be remembered.

Key skills: Memory training, concentration and visualisation
skills.

67 Jumbled up games   *7–11+ years*

We make sense of the world by translating our experiences into
words and by giving them some sort of structure and order.
Jumbled Up games challenge your child to make meaning and

order out of a confusing jumble of words and lines. Any number of people can play, though it is best played in pairs or small groups.

- **Jumbled up words**
  The game can be played using letter tiles, pencil and paper or on the computer.
  1 With letter tiles (for example tiles from a Scrabble set) or with letters written separately on cards, you can use either capital or lower case letters.
  2 Choose letters that make up a word your child knows well, such as a name (eg MICHAEL) and jumble them into a funny order (eg LACEHIM).
  3 Players try to sort out the letters into a meaningful word. Let your child jumble up some words to challenge you or his friends.

- **Jumbled up rhymes and poems**
  1 Print out a short rhyme or poem your child knows and cut it up into separate lines.
  2 Challenge your child to put the lines into the right order (or an order which makes sense).
  Move on to playing with rhymes and poems your child does not know. Can he make the jumbled lines make sense?

- **Jumbled up picture book**
  Copy the pages of a picture book that your child knows, shuffle them up and see if your child can put them into an order that makes sense.

- **Jumbled up story**
  Write the plot of a story your child knows well in as few lines as possible. Jumble up the order of the lines and challenge your child to put them in an order that makes sense.

Invent your own jumbled up game using recipes, instructions or the key moments in a person's life story.

Key skills: Creativity and language skills.

68 Who is it?   *7–11+ years*

This is a guessing game in which a person is described under a number of headings and players try to work out who it is. Any number can play and all that is needed is pen or pencil and paper. Children often like to play this with a partner.

- **Who is it?**

  Explain how you can describe people as being like other things, for example a season, an animal, a colour or a piece of furniture. Give some examples, such as 'She is like the sun in summer, a sleek cat and a red rug.' Once your child has the idea the guessing game can begin.

  1 One player thinks of someone that everybody else knows (eg someone in the room) but does not say who it is (or look at them!)

  2 The other players try to work out who it is by asking questions such as:

  'What kind of furniture is this person?'
  'What kind of animal?'
  'What sort of shop?'
  'What kind of holiday?'

  The player who has chosen the mystery person must answer the question to give a clue to whom it is.

  3 The person who guesses correctly can be the next to think of someone, or everyone who wants can have a turn.

  Other kinds of people to choose might be TV or story characters, relatives or classmates that everyone knows.

- Who is being drawn?
    1 A simpler version is simply for one player to draw their chosen person on a large sheet of paper that all can see.
    2 The first to guess who it is from the emerging drawing wins that round.
    3 They then draw their mystery person or take turns.

Key skills: Creativity, verbal fluency and language skills (making similes and metaphors)

69 Rhyming tennis   *7–11 years*

This simple game can be played anywhere. It is called 'rhyming tennis' because rhymes are batted to and fro between the players.

- **Rhyming tennis**
    1 Two players or pairs of players take turns to say rhyming words, for example 'say', 'grey', neigh' (the word must end with the same sound but not necessarily the same spelling). The youngest player starts and the game continues until one player or pair cannot think of a rhyming word. A rhyming word can only be used once in any round. The player who says the last rhyming word is the winner.
    2 The player or team that loses begins the next round.
    3 Any disputes about whether a word is a true rhyme can be settled with a dictionary or someone who will be an umpire.
    Half rhymes (words which nearly rhyme such as 'wet' and 'eat') are not allowed. Nor are sight rhymes (words that end in the same letter but sound different, such as 'move' and 'love')

- **Rhyming couplets**
    In this game players say a line and the next adds a line ending

with a rhyming word. Two rhyming lines are called a couplet
of the form AABB.

1 The first player makes up the first line of the couplet such
   as 'There was a boy who never went to school',
2 The next must think up a line that rhymes, for example:
   'He wasn't very clever, but he thought he was cool.'
3 The first players create the next line, for example; 'One day
   he drove his teacher mad.' The lines can be silly but must
   make some kind of sense, for example the next player said:
   'When the boy told the others the teacher was his dad.'

Later try other rhyming patterns such as rhyming alternate
lines (ABAB)

See also the rhyming game p63.

Key skills: Verbal fluency and language skills (awareness of
sound patterns or phonemes).

70 Listening games   *6–11+ years*

Give your child interesting things to listen to and make it a
game in which he has to identify mystery sounds which could be
sounds you make while his eyes are closed, or sound effects on a
CD. Play listening games with groups of children, such as:

• **Mystery voices**
  Players take turns to identify people by the sound of their
  voices. The game makes players experiment with the sound of
  their voice and calls for attentive listening.
  1 The first player faces a wall, with eyes closed and must not
     look round.
  2 A player is chosen (or volunteers) to be the 'mystery voice'.
     They stand well away from the first player, and on a signal

greet the first player in a disguised voice, saying for example: 'Hello Julie'.

3 The first player guesses who the mystery voice belongs to. They can ask the 'mystery voice' to repeat what they said again. The player is allowed only one guess.

4 If they guess right they win, if not the mystery player wins. Each player is given a turn, if they wish, to be a mystery voice. Encourage them to use as a strange voice. Let them practice their 'mystery voices' for a few minutes before the game starts.

- **Chinese whispers**
  This game needs several players, who sit in a circle.
  1 The first player thinks of a message and whispers it to the next player.
  2 The second player whispers it to the third player who whispers it to the next player and so on round the circle until it returns to the first player.
  3 The first player then says what the message has become and what it was when it started.
  The group wins if the message is the same at the ends as the beginning. The versions can end up being very different!

Key skills: Listening, language and concentration skills.

71 Just a minute   *7–adult*

Players must speak continuously for just a minute on a given topic. Any number can play. Two versions are given below, a simpler version for 7–9 year olds, and a harder version for 9 year olds and upwards.

- **Just a minute (simpler version)**
  In the simple version of the game players must speak for a

minute without repeating the same sentence or phrase they have used before.

1 A player, given a topic to talk about, tries to talk for one minute on this subject without repeating themselves, 'drying up' or giving up.

2 A referee times the talk.

3 The speaker wins if they succeed in talking for one minute or more.

With some children once they start talking it is hard to get them to stop, others may struggle over hard topics. Start by choosing topics your child knows best. If your child finds speaking for one minute hard try a target of half a minute.

- **Just a minute** (harder version)
  In this version players must speak for a minute on a given topic, without hesitation, deviation from the subject or repetition of any nouns, verbs or adjectives. Allow children time to think about and prepare their given topic.

Another version is to make a five minute speech on a chosen subject, or use a mobile phone:

- **Mobile chat**
  Players take turns to speak on a mobile phone to an imaginary person who has phoned them. They must speak for one minute (as above) and then pass the phone to the next player saying there is a call for them. Players win if they can keep speaking for one minute (without undue hesitation or repetition).

Key skills: Language, quick thinking and creative thinking skills

72 Name games

These question and answer name games are good for car journeys.

- **The alphabetical name game**
  You ask the questions and your child must think of things beginning with the same letter or letter sound. Each round features words beginning with the next letter of the alphabet, starting with 'A'. For example:

  Q: 'What's your name?'
  A: 'My name is Angel'
  Q: 'Where do you live?'
  A: 'I live in Alaska'
  Q: 'What do you eat?'
  A: 'I eat apples'

  Other starter questions could include: 'What's your favourite animal?' 'What do you like to drink?' 'What do you like to wear?' 'What is your favourite game?' 'What job do you do?' etc. Vary the game with other names, for example; 'My name is Boris'. 'Where do you live?' 'I live in Belgium' and so on.

- **Alphabetical travelling**
  Each player asks the next player three questions:

  'Who are you?'
  'Where are you going?'
  'What will you do there?'

  The replies must include the name of a person, a place and a description of an activity, for example 'Pat' 'Panama' and 'Plant perfect peaches'. Each word in the answers must begin with the same letter. The first player's answers begin with 'A', the next 'B' and so on through the alphabet. Allow time for your child to think before they reply.

Key skills: Language (vocabulary and alphabet) and creative thinking skills

73 Story games   *6–11+ years*

Story games help develop language skills, oral ability and quick thinking and any number can play.

- **Story chain**
  To make a story chain each person playing must continue the story in turn, but may stop at any point they choose.
  1 Players sit facing each other. One player is chosen, or volunteers to begin the story.
  2 The storyteller (who could be an adult or child) can stop at any point, even mid-sentence and the next player must continue the story from there.
  3 This player stops at any time and the next continues the story, and so on.
  4 Players who pause too long or cannot continue are out of the game.
  Play continues until the story ends or all are too exhausted to continue. Variations of the game include each player adds only one sentence to the story each time, each player must finish in mid-sentence and the storyteller chooses the next to continue by passing a ball, shell or other token to them.

- **Story picture**
  For this game you will need a collection of pictures, for example pages cut from colour magazines. The game can be played by individuals or in pairs.
  1 The first player (or pair) chooses a picture from the collection.
  2 They look at the picture and make up a story about it, referring to some of the visual elements.

A variation on the game is to choose two pictures and make up a story which links both pictures or choose 3 or more pictures illustrating episodes in the same story. Ask your child to think about what might have happened before, during and after what is shown in the picture.

- **Story sequence**
  Cut out about six pictures from a story in a book or comic. Mix them up and see if your child can put them into an order and make a story from them. It does not matter if they are put in the same order as in the book or comic – the aim is to create imaginative stories with a beginning, middle and end.

Key skills: Language, visual and creative thinking skills

74 Maze games   *6–11+ years*

Mazes are great fun to get lost in and to try to find your way out. Visit a local maze, or the one at Hampton Court. Share the famous maze story involving Theseus and the monster called the Minotaur with your child. Show your child some books of mazes to look at together.

- **Draw a maze**
  Make up your own maze and get your child to draw one.
  1 Look at some pictures of mazes and find your favourites.
  2 Draw your own maze for your child to try to find a way through. If you find this difficult copy and adapt a picture of an existing maze. Your child will probably be more interested in a maze you have drawn than one in a book.
  3 Encourage your child to try drawing their own mazes for you or friends to find a way through.

- **Word maze**

  A word maze is a maze made out of a word through which your child must find as many routes as possible. For this you will need a pen or pencil and paper.

  1 Draw the following word square to show your child

Fig 9

  2 Ask your child to trace the word 'HOLIDAY' in as many routes as possible through the maze going up and down, backwards, forwards, or diagonally, but with the pencil never leaving the paper and never going outside the squares.

Try making up your own word maze games. See also *Topological* p160.

Key skills: Visual, spatial and topographical skills.

75 Map games   *6–11+ years*

We are all familiar on a car journey with the cry 'Are we nearly there yet?'

Here are some games to play before you go to help develop your child's geographical, mathematical and map-reading skills.

Introduce maps by making a game of locating places on a

simple map, for example ask him to find a certain street or town for you. When he can do this ask him 'What towns do I go through to get from x to y?' Remember to give him clues to help him out.

Draw a map of the neighbourhood around your house, showing familiar roads. Get him to help you to add local features. See if he can go out and find a house you have marked on the map.

Ask your child to estimate how far it is from one place to another. Begin by getting him to estimate distances at home. It works well if there are two children to make the estimates so they can see who was nearest. Encourage your child to estimate, that is think about how far it might be in relation to a distance he already knows like a ruler or metre stick, not just to make wild guesses. Draw a plan of your house (and garden if you have one) or look at an estate agent's plan. Hide a secret 'treasure' for your child to find by giving clues or a map.

If you are planning a journey play the game *How far?*

- **How far?**
  1 Show your child a map showing where you are and where your destination is. Look at similar distances between places on the map and the key to the map size. Explain the difference between the distance 'as the crow flies' and the usually longer, more circuitous route of a road.
  2 Each person in the game estimates how far the journey will be.
  3 On arrival see who estimated the closest to the actual distance travelled.

See also *Estimation* p159.

Key skills: Map-reading, geographical, numerical and spatial skills.

76 Hand games   *7–11 years*

There are many games for which all you need are hands. These games require hand-eye co-ordination and manipulative skill. If you are stuck somewhere with nothing to do try playing some hand games.

- **Scissors-paper-stone**
  This is the traditional Japanese game of 'jan-ken-pon'.
  1 Each player, on a given signal, brings one hand quickly from behind their back either in the shape of scissors, paper or stone.
  2 The two players then compare their hands to see which shape has won.
  3 Scissors cut and so beats paper, paper wraps and so beats stone, and stone blunts and so beats scissors.
  The winner is of course the one who best anticipates what his opponent is going to do, so there is some psychology as well as assessing probabilities involved in the game.

- **Catch it**
  This simple game tests your child's speed of reaction.
  1 Ask your child to stand with arms outstretched in front of them with hands about 20cm apart. Hold in the air a small light object, such as a matchbox, over your child's hands.
  2 Tell them that the object of the game is for them to catch the box (or object).
  3 Wait for a while to build up tension, and then drop it without warning.
  Most children try to clap their hands together to catch the object – and miss. But they may work out a better way to catch it . . .

- **Jacks**
  Jacks was played in ancient Greece using knucklebones. Five small stones can act as 'jacks'. The aim is to throw one in the air and pick up another before catching it. When this can be done try picking up two or more, or move others round, before catching it. Try inventing some increasingly difficult moves.

Make up some of your own versions of these games.

Key skills: Hand-eye co-ordination, manipulative skill and anticipation.

77 Target numbers   *7 years–adult*

The aim of these games is to pick up number cards that add to a target number. Playing them will help develop understanding of number and require some strategic thinking.

- **Target fifteen**
  For this game you will need a row of 9 squares or cards labelled with the numbers 1–9. The aim is to make a total of 15 out of three number cards.
  1 Players take it in turns to choose one number square from a line of cards numbered 1–9.
  2 The winner is the player who takes three cards that add up to fifteen.
  It may help to go over with your child all the ways of making 15 before the game begins.

- **Target twenty five**
  For this you need a set of 14 cards or squares numbered 2–15
  1 Players take it in turns to choose one number square from the line of cards.

2 The winner is the player who takes cards that add up to twenty five.

- **Target 100**
  Players need pen or pencil and paper.
  1 The first player writes any number from 1 to 10 on a piece of paper.
  2 The next player writes any number from 1 to 10, and adds the two numbers together.
  3 Players continue to choose a number between 1 and 10, in turn, and add it to the running total.
  4 The player who adds their number to the total to make the target number of 100 is the winner.
  Try to invent your own variation of the game. With an older child investigate ways of making 100 using the digits 1–9 and mathematical symbols.

- **Card target**
  Use a pack of playing cards with court cards (jacks, queens and kings) removed.
  1 Lay 36 cards down in a 6 × 6 square. Make the target number by turning over two of the remaining cards and adding their numbers.
  2 Each player tries to spot and grab any two cards which add up to the target number.
  3 The player who picks up most cards wins.
  Play later rounds using 3 and then 4 of the spare cards to make the target number.

See also *Number battle* p158.

Key skills: Understanding of number and strategic thinking.

78 Count down   *7 years–adult*

This is a co-operative problem-solving game, in which all players try to solve a puzzle. The aim is to get all numbers in a single column in the countdown order of 9–8–7–6–5–4–3–2–1, with 9 at the top and 1 at the bottom. For this game you will need number cards or counters marked 1–9, and a chart with 3 columns.

- **Count down**
  1. Place the number cards face down and shuffle them, then choose and place three of the cards in each column and turn them face up to reveal their numbers.
  2. Players take turns to move one number card at a time from the bottom of one column to the bottom of another column. A number card can only be moved under a card with a lower number, but if a column is empty any card can be placed at the head of it.
  3. When the numbers have been placed in a single column in the countdown order of 9–8–7–6–5–4–3–2–1 the puzzle is solved and the players are winners. If they fail they to do this they lose (but note there is a way to win no matter how stuck you seem!)

If you succeed try to solve the puzzle from other starting positions, or make up your own variation on the game.

Key skills: Problem solving, perseverance, and co-operation.

79 Pig!   *7 years–adult*

Pig is a lively dice game involving numbers and probability. You will need pen or pencil and paper and one or more dice.

- **Pig!**

  The winner is the player who reaches a target score, for example 50 or 100.

  1 On their turn players may throw the dice as many times as they like until they decide to stop, each throw adding to their score. But if a one is thrown it ends the player's turn and his whole score for that turn is lost. Players may then shout 'Pig!'

  2 Players take turns to throw the dice and add the points they get to their total. If they throw a one of course they do not add any points to their score.

  3 The player to reach the target score first is the winner.

  The player who starts first has an advantage. One way of evening the advantage is for all the players to have the same number of turns. The fairest way to play is to organise it so that in a series each player has a turn to play first. Or you may decide that the youngest should start (for other ways of choosing who starts see p8).

Vary the rules to make your own dice game.

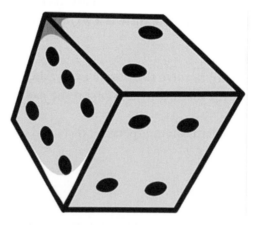

Fig 10

Discuss with your child the probability of throwing a one with the dice (the odds are 6–1). Explain that whatever numbers have been thrown the odds always remain 6–1. Experiment to see if you can show this in a large number of throws.

Key skills: Understanding of numbers and probability

80 Race games   *6 years–adult*

Many traditional board games such as Snakes and Ladders and Ludo involve a race. Try making up your own race games, like the ones that follow.

- **The cat and mouse game**
  For this game you need a dice, two counters and a large piece of paper or card. On the card draw a race track 20 squares long in any shape you like (mark square 20 as the mouse's hole). Cut out a cat and a mouse shape from card (or use two counters to represent the cat and mouse). The aim of the game is to try to predict whether the cat will catch the mouse before it escapes down a hole.
  1 Start by placing the cat at square one, and the mouse at square ten.
  2 Before the game ask your child to predict what he thinks will happen: 'Do you think the cat will catch the mouse or will the mouse escape?'
  3 Players take turns to move the cat or the mouse according to the number thrown on the dice. If 1, 2, 3 or 4 are thrown the mouse moves that number of squares towards his hole. If 5 or 6 are thrown the cat moves that number towards the mouse.
  4 If the mouse reaches square 20 or beyond he escapes down his hole. If the cat reaches the same square as the mouse, or beyond, the mouse is caught and loses the race.

5 When the race is over, the player(s) who predicted the out-
come correctly wins the game.
Try varying the rules of the game by changing the distances
the cat and mouse must move, or the numbers on the dice
that allow them to move. The following is another version of
the game.

• **The hare and the tortoise**
Draw a race track 20 squares long. The tortoise and hare may
be represented by card shapes or any two objects. They start
side by side and must reach square 20 to win. The tortoise
moves if 1, 2, 3 or 4 is thrown. The hare moves if 5 or 6 is
thrown. Can you predict who will win?
Try varying the rules of the game.

Key skills: Probability, experiment and prediction.

81 Strategy games

Strategy games encourage your child to use logical and strategic
thinking including thinking ahead and predicting. These games
require a collection of small objects such as counters, coins or
matchsticks, as well as pen or pencil and paper. Any number can
play as individuals or pairs.

• **Take the last**
The winner of this game is the one who takes the last counters from the table
1 Place a pile of small objects on a flat surface. Decide the
maximum number that can be taken in any one go, for
example ten. Decide who goes first.
2 The first player takes any number of objects from the pile
up to the agreed maximum.

3 Players take turns to remove objects from the pile (from one to the maximum number).

4 The player who takes the last objects is the winner.

Play variations on this game, for example when the player who takes the last object is the loser, or with different numbers of objects taken from the pile. Here is another variation:

- **Poison!**

  You need ten objects such as counters, coins or matchsticks, or pencil and paper .

  1 Place the counters in a row (or draw them on paper). Players can take one or two counters from anywhere in the row. The last counter left is 'poison' and the player left with it loses.

  2 The first player takes one or two counters from anywhere in the row.

  3 The second player does the same and players take turns to pick up one or two counters.

  4 The player left with the last counter (the 'poison') is the loser.

Give your child some clues to the best strategy by asking: 'If you leave one for the other player you win. Who wins if you leave two/three/four etc.) Hint: The person who leaves four or seven should win every time. Try playing some variations of this game for example using up to 20 counters, only taking one or two that are next to each other. See also *Nim* p162.

Key skills: Logic, strategic thinking, problem solving, planning and predicting.

82 Achi   *6–9+ years*

Achi is a simple board game for two players, popular in West African countries, particularly Ghana. A board can be easily drawn on a piece of paper or cardboard, or can be scratched in the sand on a beach using some pebbles as counters. You will need a board and four black and four white counters, or other colours (see fig 11).

- **Achi**

  The aim of the game is to be the first player to get three counters in a row.

  1 Players take turns to put one counter on any of the nine points on the board. They must try to get three of their counters in a row (vertical, horizontal or diagonal), while preventing the other player from doing the same.

  2 Once all eight counters are on the board (assuming no player got three in a row), there should be only one vacant point.

  3 Players take turns to move one of their counters one place to the next vacant point along a line. Play continues until one player wins by getting three counters in a row.

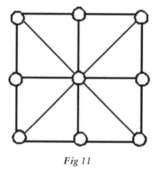

Fig 11

Key skills: Strategy, planning and problem solving.

83 Three in a row   *7 years to adult*

This is one of the oldest board games in the world. It was played by ancient Egyptians, Roman soldiers and Vikings and was popular in medieval times. The board consists of three squares whose sides

are connected with lines, as in the diagram below. After playing Tic
tack toe (Noughts and Crosses) with your child (see p84), go on to
play these two versions of the simple strategy game.

- **Three in a row**
  The game is played with two players with four counters each
  (of different colours). If a player manages to put three in a row
  either horizontally or vertically they win.
  1 Players take turns to place their counters one at a time on
    any intersection (where two or more lines meet) on the
    board. Only one counter is allowed on any intersection.
    Each player must try to stop the other putting three in a
    row.
  2 Once players have placed their four counters on the board
    they take turns to move their counters to try to make three
    in a row either horizontally or vertically. The first player to
    succeed wins.

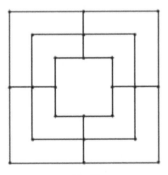

Fig 12

- **Nine Men's Morris**
  Using the same board the aim again is to place three counters
  in a line.
  1 Each player has nine counters or coins which they take
    turns in placing on any of the 24 intersections of the board.
  2 After all the counters have been placed, if there are not

three in a row, players take turns to move one counter one place to try to make three in a row.

3 When a row of three is formed either horizontally or vertically the player can remove one the other player's pieces.

4 Each time a new row of three is formed the player removes one of the other player's pieces. When a player has no more pieces left, or resigns the game, he loses.

Twelve Men's Morris (also called *Marabaraba* in South Africa) is played on a board on which four diagonal lines are added. The commercial game *Connect Four* is a modern version of the old game. See also *Achi* (p119) and *Go-muku* (p164).

Key skills: Logic, strategic thinking, problem solving, planning and predicting.

84 Drawing games   *6 years–adult*

These simple drawing games can be challenging and fun for all ages.

- **Squiggles**

  Squiggles is about taking a small beginning, a squiggle or small shape, and extending the drawing in your own way. Any number can play, for fun or in competition. Each players needs something to draw with and to draw on.

  1 One person draws a squiggle (a small shape, line or curve) in the middle of each player's paper.

  2 Players are given time to think what they might turn their squiggle into and are given a time limit, from 2–5 minutes, to do their drawing.

  3 When the players have finished, or time is up, the drawings

are shown (or judged by someone who does not know the author of each drawing),

4 Another player, or the winning player, is then invited to draw the next squiggle.

Near identical squiggles can turn into amazingly different finished drawings. Vary the game by choosing a different genre such as portrait, seascape, landscape, abstract pattern, skies, still life etc. for each round of squiggle drawing. Allow coloured pens and pencils or crayons to add to the creative possibilities!

- **Circle drawing**
  The aim is to create as many different drawings as you can based on a circle shape.
  1 Prepare a page of circles (about 5cm diameter) eg by drawing round a jar lid.
  2 Players try to draw as many different things as possible in a given time using each circle, for example drawn as a face, sun, watch etc.
  3 When time is up players score 1 point for each drawing and 2 points for a drawing no-one else has drawn.
  Try the game using different shapes eg triangles, squares, ovals etc.

- **Funny folk**
  1 Each player has a piece of paper and draws the top half of a funny person, animal or monster, without showing it to other players.
  2 When players have finished they fold the paper over so only the bottom of the picture can be seen.
  3 Players swap their folded drawings with each other, then complete their given picture by drawing the bottom half of the funny person, animal or monster.
  4 When the hidden drawings are finished players unfold and reveal their drawings.

For more drawing games see p165.

Key skills: Manipulative skills, creativity and visual thinking.

85 Card games   *6 years–adult*

War and *Cheat!* are good card games for young children. See also *Snap* (p74).

- **War**
  Start by showing the ranking system of cards by laying a suit down in the correct order: 2–3–4–5–6–7–8–9–10– J–Q–K–Ace. When your child knows this they are ready to play.
  1 Deal the cards between two players face down in front of them. Players do not look at their cards. They are now ready for war!
  2 Both players turn over the top card of their pile and place it in the middle of the table.
  3 The highest ranking card wins. Aces are high and suits don't matter.
  4 If the cards are equal value, they play again and the highest rank card wins the four cards.
  The winner is the player who wins all, or the most cards.

Cards laid out in rank order

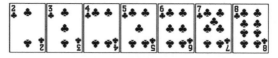

Fig13a

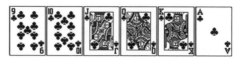

Fig 13b

- **Cheat!**

  Cheat is an easy game with plenty of scope for bluffing, cheating and trying to read the minds of others. It can be played by two or more (the more the merrier).

  1 A pack of cards is dealt out between the players. Players hide their cards from each other.

  2 The first player places one card *face down* on the table and says what its value is eg 'Four'. Players however do not have to tell the truth (it might be a 'ten' or any other card).

  3 The next player must now lay face down one or more cards that are either same value eg 'Four', or one higher eg 'Five' or one lower eg 'Three'. The player for example might say 'one four', 'two fives', 'three threes'. If they have no playable card they must bluff and play any card (or cards) pretending their cards are either four(s), fives(s) or threes(s).

  4 Players take turns in laying down cards until a player suspects another is cheating and not laying down cards that they say. The player then says 'Cheat!' If the previous player has cheated and the cards are not what they say the cheat must pick up all the cards. If the player has told the truth the player who said 'Cheat' must collect all the cards.

  5 The player who picks up the cards restarts the game.

  6 The player who gets rid of all their cards is the winner.

  Other good card games for younger children include *Beggar my Neighbour,* and *Eights.* For more card games see p167.

Key skills: Card ranking (in 'War'), strategic thinking, prediction and mind reading (in Cheat!).

86 Board games   *6 years–adult*

All board games challenge children to follow rules, to play collaboratively, and cope with winning or losing. Some rely on luck like *Snakes and Ladders*, others involve strategic thinking like *Draughts* (Checkers) and the following games:

- **Madelinette**

  Two play on a board and have 2 differently coloured counters or coins each.

  1 Draw the board (see below) and place the six counters on the points shown, leaving the middle point vacant. Decide who will go first.

  2 Each player takes turns to slide one of their counters to a vacant point on the board, with the aim of blocking the other player's counters so they cannot move.

  3 The player whose pieces are blocked and cannot move loses. Ask your child to think about where they would need to place their pieces to block your pieces.

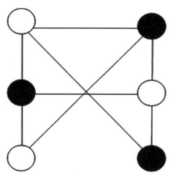

Fig 14

Key skills: Strategic thinking and spatial awareness

87 Dodgem

Noughts and crosses is often been the first simple pencil and paper strategy game that children are taught . . . However Dodgem is a more interesting strategy game for two that can be played either using noughts or crosses for each side, or other more interesting play pieces.

- **Dodgem**

  Dodgem is played on a 3 × 3 board (see fig 15), with each player having two pieces which might be counters, coins or small toys such as dinosaurs or cars. Each players' pieces are of different colours, called here Black and White. The board is set up as in the diagram. In each turn players can move one of their pieces to an empty square either left, right or forwards. The aim of the game is to move your pieces to the opposite side then off the board and to prevent the other player doing the same. However players may not block both the other player's pieces, otherwise they lose. They must always leave one square or the other player to move a piece into.

  1 White moves first and players take turns to move one piece to an empty square.

  2 The player who gets both his cars to move off the opposite side of the board wins.

  Try playing on a 4 × 4 or a 5 × 5 board (always remembering to, leave bottom left hand corner square empty.

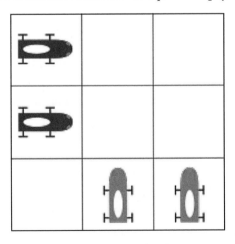

Fig 15 Dodgem board

Key skills: Strategic thinking and forward planning

88 Dotty games   *6–9+ years*

Dotty games are simple pencil and paper games which encourage strategic thinking.

Start by drawing a playing field of 16 dots, four in each direction (see fig 16).

• **Linking**
  Take turns. Link any two dots that are next to each other, side by side, above or below. A dot may be linked with only one other dot. The winner is whoever makes the last link.

• **Right up**
  Take turns. Start at the dot in the lower left hand corner. Link with a straight line as long as you like to another dot either right or above it. Each player in turn draws a line either right or up. The winner is whoever lands on the dot in the upper right hand corner.

• **Any way**
  Take turns. Join any two dots with a line (across, up, down or diagonally). A line must never cross another line, or close a shape. Your line must be drawn from either end of a line already there in straight lines only. The winner is whoever draws the last line.

• **Four square**
  Take turns. One player marks **X**s, the other uses **O**s. Mark any dot with an **X** (or **O**). The winner is the player who can mark four dots that would make a square (if connected). The winner connects their dots into a square.

Once you have played these try adding more dots, and make up your own rules.

For more dotty games see p77.

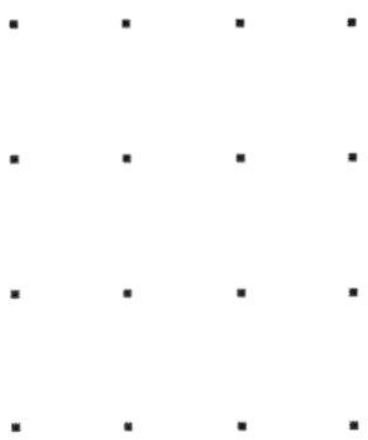

Fig 16 Dotty games

Key skills: Strategic thinking and topological skills

89 Tongue Twisters   *6 years–adult*

Tongue twisters are great fun and give your child good practice in quick speaking and thinking as well as developing word skills for example Winnie the Pooh's: 'Help, help a Heffalump, a Horrible Heffalump' or 'The sixth sheikh's sixth sheep is sick'.

- **Tongue Twisters**
  Introduce your child to some of the most famous tongue twisters, but only do it one at a time so that he has time to practice and maybe discuss what the meaning of the words.

  Greek grapes.
  Red lorry, yellow lorry.
  Unique New York.
  Freshly-fried flying fish.
  Which wristwatches are Swiss wristwatches?
  Peter Piper picked a peck of pickled peppers./ Did Peter Piper pick a peck of pickled peppers?

If Peter Piper Picked a peck of pickled peppers,/ Where's the peck of pickled peppers Peter Piper picked?

She sells seashells by the seashore./ The shells she sells are surely seashells./ So if she sells shells on the seashore,/ I'm sure she sells seashore shells.

How much wood would a woodchuck chuck/ If a woodchuck could chuck wood?/ He would chuck, he would, as much as he could,/ And chuck as much as a woodchuck would/ If a woodchuck could chuck wood.

Moses supposes his toeses are roses,/ but Moses supposes erroneously;/ for nobody's toeses are poses of roses,/ as Moses supposes his toeses to be.

Many an anemone sees an enemy anemone.

Imagine an imaginary menagerie manager/ imagining managing an imaginary menagerie.

The epitome of femininity.

A skunk sat on a stump and thunk the stump stunk,/ but the stump thunk the skunk stunk.

He stood on the balcony, inexplicably mimicking him hiccupping, and amicably welcoming him home.

Make up your own tongue twister by putting words together beginning with the same letter. Challenge your child to make up his own tongue twister to try on you!

Key skills: Verbal and thinking skills.

90 Domino games   *6 years–adult*

Dominoes began in ancient China where they marked patterns of round dots on bones and tiles and played games with them. Later these developed into dominoes. A traditional set of dominoes has 28 tiles made of wood or plastic, with spots on each end, which goes from a zero (blank) to six spots at each end (double six).

Young children often begin by having fun by trying to build, balance and topple them over. Playing domino games will help him learn about matching numbers, putting things in sets, patterns and shapes.

- **Domino patience**
  This is a great game for teaching your child how to play dominoes.
  1 Place all the dominoes face down and shuffle them.
  2 Choose five dominoes, turn them over and place on in the middle of the table.
  3 Look to see if any of the others has the same number of pips as the one just played. If so join the dominoes with matching numbers of pips to each other, for example 3 pips next to 3 pips (see fig 17). For each of the 5 dominoes you play you pick another to replace it from the remaining dominos.
  4 Try to join as many of the others to make a chain, always keeping only five dominos on show.
  5 Keep playing until you have played all the dominoes or cannot go. You win if you can use all the dominoes.
  Make the game easier by choosing six or seven dominoes. Play the game with two or more players by giving each having a hand of five, six or seven dominoes and playing in turns. The first player to get rid of all his dominoes is the winner.

- **Seven up**
  A game for two or more players played by joining matching numbers, as above. Points are awarded to players who make the matching ends add up to seven.
  1 Dominoes are placed face down, shuffled and each player takes seven dominoes.
  2 Take turns to play by matching the ends of each domino played. Add a point to your score if the pips at the two ends add up to seven.

3 The player who gets rid of all his dominoes adds to his score the number of pips that are on all the dominoes that other players still have.

After several games the winner is the player with most points.

- **Threes and Fives**

  These games are played as above but you get points if the ends, in *Threes* add up to a multiple of three ie 3, 6, 9, or 12. (3 = 1 point, 6 = 2 points, 9=3 points, 12=4 points).

  In *Fives* you get a point if the ends add up to a multiple of five (5=1 point, 10=2 points, 15=3 points). Note: It is usual to play doubles eg double five across the matching number (five) as in fig, allowing the end tiles to add up to 15 or even 20.

Make up your own rules and variations and play in ways that suit you and your child best!

Fig 17

Key skills: Matching, strategy and number skills.

4

Brain Games for your older child
(9+ years)

In your child's final phase of childhood before he reaches adolescence he is becoming much more aware of himself as a person and developing an ability to use and understand abstract ideas until a near-adult level is reached by adolescence. He becomes capable of understanding complex ideas and to play abstract games like chess, though he will still enjoy playing many of the games he played when younger and the games that younger brothers and sisters enjoy.

Give your older child opportunities to develop real skills such as cooking, sewing, and making things. Support your child's interest in the world around him. Encourage him to participate in an organized club or youth group. Many groups encourage skill development with projects or activities and introduce new social games.

Remember also to provide time and space for an older child to be alone, to read, daydream, or do school work uninterrupted. Encourage your older child to help you with younger children, but avoid burdening him with too many adult responsibilities. He still needs to be nourished with stories and with the mental stimulus of conversation and play. These are games for thinking about and talking about as well as playing for fun. Encourage him to play games of strategy like draughts (checkers), Monopoly as well as a trying out many other brain games that will help him prepare for the challenge of adolescence (see games 91 –120) Talk to him about playing with a *strategy*, that is thinking of a plan that might result in winning. Introduce him to the best strategy game of them all – chess. Whatever brain game you play encourage him to play in a thoughtful way and not to rely just on luck.

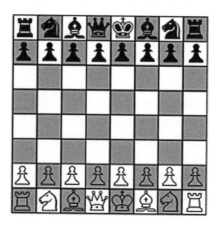

Fig 18 Chess board

Brain games for your older child (9+ years)

91 Word links
92 What am I thinking of?
93 Origami Book
94 Crazy answers
95 Categories
96 Speed word
97 Book race
98 Memory games: Pelmanism
99 Rhyming consequences
100 Questioning games

91 Word links   *9–12 years*

Word links is about making connections between a group of words. It can be played with one or more children. You will need a board or paper to write on and some pens or pencils.

- **Word links**
  1 Players are asked to suggest any words that come into their heads. They must be concept words, that is words that stand for something, like 'tree' or 'book', not connecting words like prepositions (such as 'under'), conjunctions (such as 'and') or indefinite articles (such as 'the').

2 Write the words on a board or large piece of paper for all to see, about 10 or 12 words is best, for example 'head', 'flower', 'tree', 'egg', 'book', 'summer', 'people', 'dream', 'football', 'dog', 'hat'.

3 Players think about the words and try to pair up any two or three words with a connecting idea, such as 'head' and 'hat'. Ask players to explain exactly what they think the connection is between the words.

4 They can draw lines to link the connected words or make a list of them. Keep playing until ideas or interest fades.

Extend the game by trying to connect three or more words or creating larger sets of words.

- **Story links**
  Collect a set of words as above, and write them on a board or paper for all to see. The challenge of this game is for each player to make up a story that uses every word in the list.
  See also *Connect* (p95), and *Crazy answers* (p139).

Key skills: Creative and conceptual thinking, language skills.

92 What am I thinking of?   *9–12 years*

A game for two or more people requiring no equipment except a lively mind. It involves an attempt at 'mind-reading', trying to guess what someone is thinking then saying how your guess links with the word they were thinking of to show how your guess was right or nearly right.

- **What am I thinking of?**
  1 One player is the 'thinker' and thinks of something that exists in the world.

2 Other players guess what the thinker is thing of and each in turn says what word they think the 'thinker' is thinking of.

3 The thinker *does not respond* until all have had a guess, then says what it he or he was thinking about.

4 Each of the guessing players then tries to justify their guess by linking it in some way to what the thinker was thinking about. For example if I guessed 'flower' and the thinker was thinking of 'dinner' I might say 'I am right because there are always flowers on the dinner table'.

The fun and challenge of the game is to think up a clever way in which whatever you said links up with the thing the thinker was thinking about. Take turns in being the 'thinker'. If playing in a group the player the thinker decides made the closest link becomes the next 'thinker'.

This game can be played anywhere and is good for a long car journey.

Key skills: Language and reasoning and skills of social interaction and intuition.

93 Origami book   *9–12 years*

Your child may have had some experience of origami (for example by making the origami house p96). Origami is both an art form and a practical means of learning how to make models and beautiful wrappings. Remember to practice any origami model yourself before showing your child.

To make an origami book you will need to start with a sheet of A4 size white paper. In origami it is a good idea to have several sheets handy in case of mistakes!

- **Origami book**

  To make an origami book show your child how to fold the paper as follows:

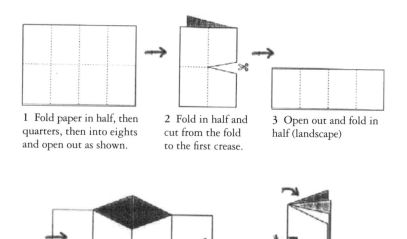

1 Fold paper in half, then quarters, then into eights and open out as shown.

2 Fold in half and cut from the fold to the first crease.

3 Open out and fold in half (landscape)

4 Push the ends inwards to form a cube.

5 Push the ends together to flatten the cube, then fold the pages around to form a book.

Fig 19 Stages in making origami book

Make sure the folds are firm and the cut with the scissors is done carefully.

Once the 'book' is made it can be decorated and the pages filled with writing, drawing or cut-outs.

Key skills: Manipulative dexterity, creativity and ability to follow instructions.

94 Crazy answers   *9–12 years*

Crazy answers challenges your child's to think creatively and all you needed is a pen or pencil and pieces of paper.

- **Crazy answers**
  Each player is given three pieces of paper, one for writing a question, the next for writing a noun and the third is left blank for the answer (alternatively you can prepare a collection of slips of paper with a question or a noun on each). The aim of the game is to answer the question using the noun as part of the answer.
  1 On their first slip of paper each player writes any question they like.
  2 On the second piece they write a noun or noun phrase.
  3 The slips of paper with the questions are put into a box or hat and shuffled, and each player then chooses (or is given) a question.
  4 The nouns are then shuffled and each person chooses one.
  5 The players, individually or in pairs, must then make up a crazy answer to the question, on their third slip of paper. Their answer must include the noun they have been given.
  6 Questions and answers are then read out, and everyone thinking of an answer using their noun that makes some kind of sense is a winner!

The following is an example; the question on the paper was 'Why do mice eat cheese?' The noun that was picked out was 'blue'. The answer a child wrote was: 'Mice like to eat cheese because if they did not they would be hungry and that would make them feel blue!'

Key skills: Language skills, creative thinking and verbal reasoning

95 Categories   *9–12 years*

In this game players try to list as many words within given categories as possible. Any number can play, though children often prefer to play in pairs or teams. It can be played verbally or with paper and pencil.

- **Categories**
  1 Players begin by choosing a letter. (Choose a letter for example by asking your child to turn to a page in a book and blindly point at a word).
  2 Players then choose a category of things, for example animals, food, clothes, boys' names, girls' names, place names, book titles, TV programmes and so on.
  3 The chosen letter is the target letter for which every word in a category.
  4 Players try to think of as many words in that category beginning with the target letter. For example if the letter was 'b' and the category 'food' the list might include banana, beans or banoffi pie. If playing with pencil and paper these words are written down.
  5 When time is up or no more words can be thought of the game ends.

In the written version players score 1 point for every word and 2 points for any word not thought of by others. In each round a new letter is chosen. Either the same category can be used or a new one chosen. A variation on the category game is called Guggenheim:

- **Guggenheim**
  1 Players write a list of categories down the side of the page.
  2 They choose a name and write the letters of that name across the top.

3 Under each letter players must find a word for each category, within a time limit.

4 The first players to succeed win.

L   *A*   *U*   *R*   *A*

Animals
Clothes
Drinks
Countries

Key skills: Quick thinking, vocabulary and verbal fluency skills.

96 Speed word   *9–12 years*

The aim of the game is to define a set of words in a given time. The game will help develop your child's skills in defining words and thinking quickly. Ideally it needs three or five players, two to play (or two teams of two players) and one timekeeper.

To play you will need to prepare one or more lists of 10–15 words that denote common objects, for example: flower, tree, clock, train, light, horse, orange, bus, jam, fish, apple, beach, summer, camel, clown. A timekeeper needs a watch or clock with a second hand to keep time.

- *Speed word*

  The game involves one player defining a word, without saying what the word is and the other player trying to guess the word from the definition he has been given. For example if the definition given is: 'It is yellow, long and has a bendy shape and you can eat it.' The correct word would probably be: 'Banana'.

  1 One player (or one in each team) is given a list of words, which they must not show their partner.

2 When the timekeeper gives the signal the person with the list has to describe the word, without using the word, and his partner has to try to guess the word. If his partner cannot get the right word the first player can continue trying tom define the word or move on to the next.

3 They are given a time limit, say two minutes, to try to guess every word on their list or as many words as they can.

4 At the end of the game the players change roles and play again with a new list of words. How many words can be guessed in two minutes?

Variations on the game include using a list of verbs, or adjectives instead of nouns to be guessed. Play the game by the player with the list miming instead of using words. Place a word limit on definitions, such as the children only being able to use 5 words or less. Try making up your own speed word games.

Key skills: Quick thinking, vocabulary and verbal fluency skills

97 Book race   *9–12 years*

It is often difficult to get children to look things up, for example in dictionaries, encyclopaedias or map-books. But making a game of it can help and give them useful practice in finding things out from reference books (or other sources of information).

To play *Book race* you will need a copy of the same reference book for each player. The game will improve the speed and skill of your child in using reference books, as well as helping him to find new knowledge. The game can be played with one, but is better when two or more are competing with each other.

- *Dictionary race*

  Each player is given a reference book such as a dictionary.

  1 Someone chooses and calls out a word.
  2 The player(s) race to find the word in their reference book or dictionaries.
  3 The first player to find the word and read out the definition is the winner.

An alternative version is to ask the player(s) to find as quickly as they can a two letter, three letter, four letter, five letter word and so on, beginning with a certain letter. Invent other kinds of words to hunt, such as words ending in 'ology'. Have a one minute hunt for the longest word in a dictionary or other book, or the longest word beginning with . . . (a given letter).

Discuss with your child the quickest way of finding a word in a dictionary (or other reference source). Play book race games using different reference sources such as:

- dictionaries
- encyclopaedia
- the Bible or other religious text
- map books or atlases to find countries, oceans, cities, streets, rivers
- phone book
- computer
- library

The game is best kept short and played regularly.

Key skills: Skimming, scanning, use of reference books, research and language skills

98 Memory games   *9+ years*

Memory games are good for improving your child's memory, and
his ability to concentrate and to visualise things in the 'mind's
eye'. One of the best is *Pelmanism*:

- **Pelmanism**
  Pelmanism is a memory game played with a pack of cards.
  These could be playing cards or any pack of picture cards or
  postcards. Any number can play.
  1 Lay all the cards face up on a table or floor, so that all the
     players can see and try to remember them, for about one
     minute.
  2 Turn all the cards face down.
  3 Players take turns to choose a card. They must name or
     describe it before turning it over to see if they have cor-
     rectly identified it.
  4 If they have correctly identified the card they keep it and
     can choose again from the cards that are face down, remem-
     bering to identify what it is before turning it over. If they
     identify a card wrongly it is simply turned over again.
  5 Players take turns until all the cards are taken. The player
     with most cards at the end wins the game.

- **Turn over the pairs**
  Turn over the pairs is a variation on *Pelmanism*. The game is
  played like *Pelmanism* but players must choose and identify
  two cards (pairs) at a time. Vary the game in other rounds by
  asking them to identify three cards (trios) or four cards (quar-
  tets).

- **Which cards have moved?**
  In this memory game lay a random group of cards face up on
  the table for all to see. Players then hide their eyes (or turn

around) while you swap the positions of some of the cards. Players then must see if they can spot the differences.

See also *Kim's game* (p99).

Key skills: Memory skills, visualisation and concentration.

99 Rhyming consequences   *9 years–adult*

This is a game for children experienced with rhymes and builds on the rhyming games on p66 and p103. The aim of the game is to produce some surprising four-line verses (quatrains). Any number can play individually or in pairs. They will need a pen or pencil and paper.

The game is based on the popular 'consequences' drawing game, where players draw a head, fold the paper over for the next player to draw the body, then fold it over and pass it on to the next player who completes the legs and feet of the strange creature or person that has been drawn in three parts.

- **Rhyming consequences**
  1 Each player or team writes the opening line of a poem near the top of a blank piece of paper, then folds the paper over so no-one can see what is written. They then write the final word of their line at the bottom of the paper. This will be the end rhyming word of the next line.
  2 The folded papers are swapped between players. The next player must not see what has been written and must write the next line with the last word rhyming with the word written at the bottom of the page.
  3 The process is repeated until four lines have been written.
  4 The papers are returned, unfolded and the four lines read out.

When play begins again players might want to vary the game by trying a longer poem, altering the rhyme pattern to ABAB or allowing players to see the previous line before composing their own. Players might be allowed to use a Rhyming Dictionary to help find rhymes for difficult words.

Read some books of Nonsense verse with your child, find and share your favourite silly poems.

Key skills: Creativity, rhyming and language skills.

100 Questioning games   9 *years–adult*

Questioning games gives your child practice in questioning and answering questions. Any number can play and no materials are needed.

- **Question only**
  Players try to keep a conversation going using only questions. Questions must make sense and no question may be repeated.
  1 The first player asks a question.
  2 The second player must reply with another question, for example if the first person says 'How are you feeling today?' and the second replies 'Very well thank you' he loses, but if he says 'How do you think I am feeling?' the game continues.
  3 A player loses and drops out if he does not answer with a question. If a player pauses too, long, asks a question that does not make sense or repeats a question he loses.

     One way of scoring is for every player to have three 'lives' (symbolised eg by matchsticks or tokens). Every time a player loses (see 3) he loses a 'life'. A player wins when all others have lost their 'lives'.

Fig 20

A famous 'question only' game appears at the beginning of Tom Stoppard's play *Rosencrantz and Guildenstern are Dead*.

- **How many questions?**
  Players are challenged to ask as many questions as they can about a mystery picture or object, either playing individually or in pairs. All you need are some interesting objects or pictures.
  1 An object or picture is presented. Players are given time to think. The game begins with the first player asking a question about the object or picture.
  2 The next player must ask a different question and the game proceeds like *Questions only* (see above)
  3 The player who asks the most questions is the winner.
  Players may be asked to write down their questions about the mystery object in a given time limit, with a point scored for every question and two points for any question no-one else asks.

- **Yes, no and maybe**
  The only rule of this game is that you must not use the words 'yes', 'no' or 'maybe' when you answer a question. For example if the questioner asks: 'Would you like an ice cream?' a good answer might be 'I would like an ice cream very much' but not 'Yes please'. A player loses if they say 'yes', 'no' or 'maybe' in their answer. Take turns in asking questions.

Key skills: Verbal fluency and questioning skills.

101 Pencil and paper games   *9 years–adult*

Some traditional pencil and paper games like *Boxes* are simple, others like *Battleships* are quite complex. A great game for getting children thinking about words and spelling is *Hangman*. It can be played with a pencil and paper or on a beach with a stick by any number of players.

- **Hangman**
  The aim of the game is to discover the secret word before the man on the gallows is hanged.
  1 A player thinks of a word and draws a row of dashes for each letter of the word _ _ _ _ _
  2 The other players take turns to guess a letter in the word, for example 'a' (it is best to start with vowels as there is bound to be at least one in the word).
  3 If the guessed letter is in the word it is written on the dash where it appears, eg _ _ <u>a</u> _ _
  4 If the letter appears more than once all it must be written in all the places it occurs. If the letter does not appear in the word one part of the gallows is drawn.
  5 Players try guessing the letters, or the complete word (the above example was '<u>brain</u>'), before the gallows and the man are completed (see fig 21 below).
  It is a good idea with younger children to write down the letters as they guess them so they know what letters they have used.

If the 'hangman' drawing is completed the first player wins and reveals what the secret word was. If the other players guess the word before the 'hangman' is finished they win. In this version the 'hangman' drawing has 11 elements, so players have 11 guesses. A simpler version can be made eg by adding eyes, nose, mouth, hair or fingers, to allow for more guesses. For those who do not like the idea of a hanged man, play the game using a different drawing such as an apple tree with ten 'apples'. You can also try limiting the words used to a specific category like 'science words' or words that fit any homework topic.

See also

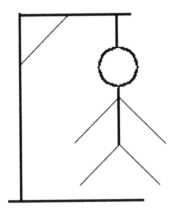

Fig 21 'Hangman' drawing

Key skills: Language, spelling and vocabulary skills

102 More memory games   *9 years–adult*

These traditional memory games can be played by any number and are easily adapted.

- **The minister's cat**
  1 The first person begins by saying 'The minister's cat is a . . . cat and his name is . . .' An adjective beginning with 'A' (for example 'angry') is said before the word 'cat' and the name given must begin with 'A' (for example 'Amy').
  2 The next person repeats these words and says again 'The minister's cat is a . . . cat and his name is . . .' (this time adding words beginning with 'B' eg 'bald' and 'Ben').

3 The next player repeats what the first and second said and adds his version with words beginning with 'C', and so on with other players going through the alphabet.

A player is out if there is too long a gap, say over ten seconds, between turns. When 'X' comes the player can use 'ex' as in 'expert'. Play can go on until 'Z' is reached when the game starts again. If a letter like 'Z' becomes too difficult then just leave it out. The winner is the player left playing at the end of the game or given time win.

- **Memory test**

  Memory test is a challenging memory game for three or more players. Begin by making a list of words numbered 1–10. Players can suggest the words while you write them down. Once you have the list you are ready to play.

  1 Ask the players to listen carefully as you read out the list with their numbers, for example 'One 'banana', two 'football', three . . .' and so on.

  2 After reading say any number from one to ten. A player who says (or writes) the word that corresponds to the number on the list gets a point.

  3 The game continues with a new number called until all the numbers up to ten have been called and see how many words the players can remember.

  4 The game can then begin again with a new list of numbered words.

Discuss ways of remembering things. For other memory games see p99.

Key skills: memory, concentration and listening skills.

103 Crosswords

9 years–adult

Crosswords is a simple but challenging game that was a favourite of Lewis Carroll. *Scrabble* and other popular word games were developed from this game. The aim of the game is to make words across and down in a crossword grid of 25 squares.

- **Crosswords**
  1 Each player is given (or draws) a blank crossword grid of 5 × 5 squares (see fig 22).
  2 The first player calls out a letter. Each player then writes that letter in any one of the squares of his crossword grid which he keeps hidden from other players.
  3 The next player chooses the next letter and each player writes this in any space on his grid.
  4 Play continues with players having turns to choose the next letter which all have to add to their grid. Each player tries to make as many words as possible which can be read either vertically (up and down) or horizontally (across).
  5 Letters are chosen until all the squares of the grid have been filled ie with 25 letters. Any letter can be chosen more than once, but no changing or rubbing out of letters is allowed.

Keep a record of the letters chosen for all to see so players can check what letters they should have used. At the end of the game grids are exchanged for marking. A good scoring system is 10 points for a 5 letter word, 5 points for a 4 letter word, 3 points for a 3 letter word and 2 points for a 2 letter word.

- **Scrabble** or Lexicon (a popular version of this game appears on Facebook)
    These classic crossword games will help develop language, strategic thinking and arithmetical skills (in adding scores). Scrabble remains an ideal brain game for any child.

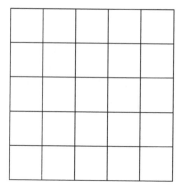

Fig 22 A longer game is to play on a 6 × 6 grid

Key skills: Vocabulary, verbal wordplay and language skills.

104 Word hunt

9 years–adult

Choose any long word or phrase and challenge your child to see
how many words he can make using only the letters that occur
in the word or phrase. The game can be played as a competition
between players or played co-operatively by pairs of players or by
you playing alongside your child. It may be helpful to let your
child have a dictionary to check on spellings.

- **Word hunt**
  1 Choose a long word such as 'Chrysanthemum' or a key phrase
     like 'Merry Christmas'. Try to choose a word or phrase with
     several vowels. Write the word out for each player.
  2 Players list all the words they can find in a given time.
     Decide beforehand whether proper nouns (eg names) or
     abbreviations are allowed. The usual rule is that only words
     found in the dictionary are allowed.
  3 At the end of the game players total up how many words
     they have found. Another way to score is to score by letter,

that is 2 points for a 2 letter word, 3 points for a 3 letter word and so on.

The game should end after a set time or when the children get bored. It will help if you give them the letters of the target word on cards or tiles so they can move them round as they try to find new words. The letters of the word 'Chrysanthemum' could for example make the words: 'mum', 'the', 'seat' and 'tummy' but not 'cherry' (as there is only one 'r' in 'Chrysanthemum')

Key skills: Creativity, vocabulary and language skills.

105 Disconnections   *9 years–adult*

This is a harder version of *Connect* (see p95). In this game players must say a word that has no connection at all with the word said before. If another player spots a connection between the two previous words they can challenge and say what the connection is. The game can be played by any number of players.

- **Disconnections**
  Choose the first player to start (for ways of choosing the first player see p8).
  1 The first player says a word. This can be any concept word, that is a word expressing an idea such as 'food' or 'holiday', not a connecting word like 'and'.
  2 The next player must then say a word that has no connection with the previous word, for example if the first word was 'apple' the next might be 'bridge'. If no-one can spot a connection between the two words the game continues.
  3 The next player must now say a word with no connection with the last word ('bridge') and so on.
  4 If a player can think of an idea that connects the last two

words they can say 'Challenge!', for example if the words
were 'bicycle' and 'train' the challenge might be they are
both forms of transport. If the challenge shows a connection
the challenger wins and the game begins again.

It is a good idea to appoint a referee or put any disputed challenge to the vote of the other players to see if they agree or not
that a true connection has been made.

Key skills: Verbal, conceptual and language skills.

106 Secret word   *9 years–adult*

Secret word is a game that helps develop logical thinking. It is
a game for two people, each requiring pen or pencil and paper.
The aim is to discover the other player's secret word.

- **Secret word**
  1 Each player writes down a secret word of four, five or six
    letters, and says how many letters it contains.
  2 The first player calls out a word containing the same
    number of letters as the other player's secret word.
  3 The second player then says how many letters this word has
    in common with his secret word. For example if the secret
    word is 'teddy' and the player guesses 'sweet', the first
    player would say 'two letters' (in this case 'e' and 't').
  4 Players take turns guessing each other's word and saying
    how many letters each guess has in common with their
    word, until one player correctly guesses what the secret
    word is.

To make the game easier each player could say the names of the
letters as well as how many are common in the two words.

- **Codes (secret messages)**

  Codes are ideal for sending secret messages.

  1 Invent a code, for example make every letter a number eg A = 1, B = 2 and so on, or make every letter represent the next letter ie A = B, B = C and so on.

  2 Make up a message for your child to decode. After a while let your child know what the code is so he can work out the secret message.

  3 Invite your child to make up a secret message for you to decode. After you have played with a few codes, give your child a secret message in a code without saying what the code is and see if he can decode it.

See also *Word logic* below.

Key skills: Logical deduction and verbal skills.

107 Word logic

9 years–adult

The aim of the game is to discover a secret word by a process of logic and deduction.

It can be played individually or in pairs and needs pen or pencil and paper.

- **Word logic**

  1 The first player chooses a four-letter word and writes it down without showing anyone.

  2 The next player's task is work out what the word might be by a series of guesses and deductions. He begins by guessing what the word might be.

  3 The first player must show how close the guess is by using these symbols:

★ star   = the correct letter is earlier in the alphabet
△ triangle = the correct letter is later in the alphabet
✕ cross   = the correct letter in the wrong place
✓ tick   = the correct letter is in the right place

The first player writes down how close the guess was using these a symbol for each letter, for example if the word was 'plan' and the guess was 'boat' the first player would write
△ ★ ✓ ★

4 The second player then guesses again using the clues he has been given.

5 Play continues until the word is guessed or the second player gives up!

Try playing the game with longer words or with a set number of turns.

Key skills: Logical deduction and verbal skills

108 Mystery numbers   *9–12 years*

For these mystery number games you will need pen or pencil and paper. They involve logical deduction and will help develop your child's understanding of number.

- **Mystery number**
  Any number can play this 'mind-reading' game of luck and skill.
  1 The first player thinks of a secret number between 0 and 100 and writes the number down in secret.
  2 The other player(s) have 10 questions to try and discover the secret number.
  3 The player with the secret number can only answer 'yes' or 'no'.

If the number is found within 10 questions that player wins, if not the first player wins and shows what the number is. Older players could try a secret number between 0 and 1000, or 10,000.

- **Hits and misses**

  Hits and misses is another game in which players must find a mystery number through a process of guesswork and deduction. Players will need a pen or pencil and paper.

  1 The first player thinks of a 4 digit secret number, for example 1952 and writes the number down in secret.

  2 The next player guesses what the number might be, saying any 4 digit number, for example 7659.

  3 The first player must show how close the guess was by saying how many hits and misses were scored. A hit means the guess contains the correct digit in the right place. A miss means the guess contains a correct digit in the wrong place. For example if the secret number was 1952, and the guess 7659, the first player would say one hit and one miss. (The hit was 5, the miss was 9, but of course he does not say this!)

  4 The second or next player uses this information to guess again. The first player then says how many hits and misses were in this guess.

  5 The game continues until a player works out what the mystery number was, or they give in and ask to see what the number was!

Try varying the rules, extending the game to 5 digits, or by giving more clues.

Key skills: Logical deduction and understanding of number

109 Number Battle   *9 years to adult*

This game involves strategic thinking and provides useful practice in mental arithmetic. The game can be played in pairs or with partners playing one side against the other. You will need pen or pencil and paper and a playing area of seven squares or circles drawn on paper and a coin (the circles can be drawn around the coin, as in fig below).

Fig 23

- **Number Battle**

  Each player starts with 100 points. The coin is placed in the middle circle or square and the aim is to move it to the other player's end circle.

  1 Players begin by writing down, in secret the number of points they wish to use in the next battle (the minimum number is 1).

  2 When both sides have written down their number, their numbers are revealed. The player, or side, with the largest number wins that battle and moves the coin forward one place towards the opponent's end.

  3 Both players, or sides, then deduct the points they have used from their total of 100. (Each side may check the arithmetic of their opponents on each turn).

  4 Play continues, as above, with each side writing down the number of points they wish to use in the next battle, the winner moving the coin one place towards their opponent's end and both sides deducting the points they have used from their remaining points.

  5 The winner is the player who moves the coin to the opponents end (that is has won three more battles than his opponent).

If one player uses up all their points, the other may have successive unchallenged turns. If both players use up all their points the game is drawn.

Key skills: Strategic thinking and mental arithmetic.

110 Estimation games *9 years to adult*

Play estimation games to develop your child's ability to make numerical assessments. Any number can play and different sorts of things will be needed with which to assess number, length, capacity and weight.

- **Estimate**
  Prepare some materials with which to challenge the players to *Estimate*, for example number of pages in a book, sweets in a packet, length of clothing or toy, weight of a bag of food, size of TV screen and so on.
  1 Show players an object such as beans in a jar, length of ribbon or the drink left in a bottle. Ask them to make an estimate in terms of a given measurement such as number, length (in centimetres), capacity (in centilitres) or weight (in grams).
  2 Allow time to think, confer and compare with other measured items such as ruler, litre of liquid or 500gram tin of food and time to make an assessment.
  3 Let players estimate several items and write their estimates down. Give them a minute for each estimation.
  4 Check the true measurements, for example by counting, weighing or measuring the true amount. The winners are those who make the nearest measurement of each object.

- **Grab**
  You will need about 200 small objects placed in a pile

between the players. In this game players are given a target, such as 35 and try to pick that number in one handful of objects from the pile. The objects grabbed are counted and the nearest to the target number wins.

Another version is to grab a pile of objects, and put them down for all to see. Can the players estimate how many are in the grabbed pile? The nearest estimate wins.

- **Size me up**
  List different parts of your child's body for him to estimate and measure, for example how many pulses or heart beats in a minute, how long is your nose, how heavy is your head?

How far are you from Paris? Are you nearer New York or Moscow? Use an atlas map or globe to estimate and measure distances between places. See also map games p110.

Key skills: Mathematical measurement, practical judgement and reasoned choices.

111 Topological games   *9 years–adult*

This is a maze game that relies on logical thinking and the ability to create different routes. This game is based on one invented by an American professor named Gale. You will need a pen or pencil and paper or prepared game board. There are 2 individual or pairs of players.

- **Topological**
  You need to draw a game board (as below). The aim of the game is to get from one side of the board to the other, either left to right (the 'o' file) or top to bottom (the 'x' file). The

problem is the other player is also trying to get from one side to the other the other way and you are trying to block each other. The winner is the first player to get across the board.

1 Players choose to cross either by the 'o' or 'x' files.
2 The player choosing the 'o' file goes first and joins two neighbouring 'o' points with a straight line.
3 The player choosing the 'x' file then joins two neighbouring 'x' points with a straight line.
4 Players take turns to continue joining a line to the previous point on their route. Lines can go in any direction. The only rule to remember is that lines must not cross.
5 The winner is the first player to make an unbroken line across the board.

The two lines will probably snake in all over the board.

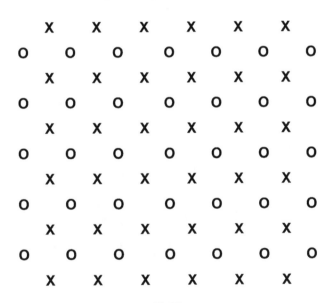

Fig 24

Topology refers to the study of the relationship between places and spaces as in maps, mazes and geometrical shapes. Try inventing a different game of topology with a different board or rules. Collect examples of mazes for your child to solve, and create your own maze puzzles together.

Key skills: Visual/spatial understanding, logical thinking and prediction.

112 Nim *9 years–adult*

This strategy game was made famous in the film *Last Year in Marienbad*. The name comes from the German word *nimmt* (take). The game is played by two players, but can be played by partners or teams.

- **Nim**
  You will need 16 counters, coins or matchsticks.
  1 Place the counters in the formation as follows:

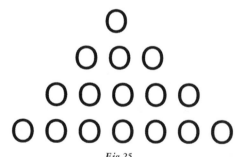

Fig 25

  2 Players take turns to remove one or more counters from any one row.
  3 The loser (or winner) is the player who picks up the last counter.

Can you find a winning strategy? Try to create your own version of the game by varying the numbers of counters in each row, or number of rows or number of counters. The following is a variation on Nim:

- **Nim 2**
  1 The 16 counters are laid out in a 4 × 4 square, as follows:

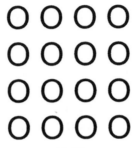

Fig 26

  2 Players take turns to take any number of counters that are next to each other from any one horizontal or vertical row. For example if a row has O O   O a player could move either of the first two (as there is a gap in the row) or the last counter.
  3 The loser (or winner) is the player who picks up the last counter.

Create your own version by varying the numbers of counters in each row, or number of rows or number of counters, for example here is a game called *Choc bar*:

- **Choc bar**
  Draw a choc bar, like the one below, with any number of square 'pieces'. Players take turns to choose and 'eat' (or cross out) either one or two pieces, starting from any piece on the outside of the bar. The loser is the player left with the last piece!

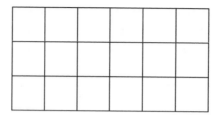

Fig 27

Key skills: Logical thinking, prediction and strategic awareness.

113 Five in a row   *9 years–adult*

This is a simple version of Japan's national game of *Go*, which was first invented in China 3000 years ago. It is the oldest board game still played regularly today. Like chess it is a game of strategy and planning. It is played by two players or by players in pairs. It requires a board drawn on paper (squared paper is good for this) or card, consisting of 19 horizontal and vertical lines (see fig 28). Traditionally each player played with 100 black or white counters, called 'stones', but in this game each player has their own colour or symbol which, when their turn comes, they draw on a square of their choice on the paper 'board'. The aim is to get five of one's own colour or symbol in a row.

- **Go-muku**

  This simpler version of *Go* is called *Go-muku*.

  1 The two players, or pairs of players, choose different colours or symbols and play on a board of squared paper of 19 x 19 lines, as shown below.

  2 Players take turns to draw their colour or symbol in an empty square.

  3 The first player to get five in a line is the winner.

  If neither side succeeds the game is drawn.

Players must try to get five in a line whilst at the same time trying to stop the other player(s) doing the same. To win may well require a lot of strategic thinking.

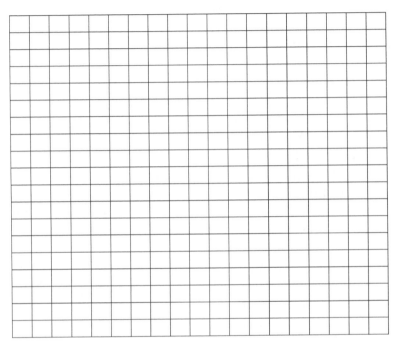

Fig 28

Key skills: Logical thinking, prediction and strategic awareness.

114 More drawing games   *9–12 years*

Some children are visual learners and love drawing, but others are not. Drawing games can help all children to develop their creative and visual skills and all that is needed is a pen or pencil and paper.

- **Drawing race**

  This is a game for two players or teams. The names of objects are written on slips of paper, for example 'pig', 'banana', 'bus', 'daffodil', 'umbrella', 'traffic lights'. An identical list is needed for each player or team. These are placed face down in front of each player or team.

  1 At a given signal one player turns over to see what is written on the first slip of paper and without showing or telling his partner draws what is written there

  2 The partner must correctly identify what the drawing represents. When they succeed the next slip is turned over and drawn as before

  3 The first player or team to draw and correctly identify all the objects wins.

  A good number of objects to draw is five. In other rounds more challenging things can be chosen to draw.

- **Blindfold drawing**

  Ask one or two players volunteer to do a drawing blindfold. They are given something to draw with and a surface to draw on such as pens and a large piece of paper, felt pens and whiteboard or chalks and a blackboard.

  1 Give the players a subject to draw, such as self-portrait, their house, their school, a cow, a vase of flowers or are shown a picture they have to copy.

  2 They are given drawing tools, shown the drawing surface and blindfolded.

  3 The blindfolded artists do their best to draw the given subject as best they can.

  4 When the player(s) have completed their drawing they stop and remove their blindfolds.

  5 Their pictures are shown, and if it is a competition, are judged (perhaps by somebody who does not know the author of each picture).

Key skills: Manipulative skills, creativity and visual thinking

115 Card games for older children ♠ ♣ ♥ ♦
9+ years

Card games can provide a never-ending source of mental stimulus and fun for people at any age. Many card games involve 'Tricks'. After learning about *Tricks*, and *Trumps*, they are ready for *Whist* and *German Whist* and later to try the most challenging game of all – *Bridge*.

- **Tricks**
  A good game for learning about 'tricks' and any number can play.
  1 Four cards are dealt to each player.
  2 The youngest player puts their highest card face up in the middle of the table eg ten of clubs.
  3 Other players take turns to place a card of that suit eg clubs on top of this card. If they do not have a card of that suit they can play any other card. The next player must again play a card of the first card's suit eg clubs.
  4 When each player has played a card, the player who played the highest card of the suit wins (see p124 for the ranking of cards). He gathers the cards and places them in a neat pile in front of him. This is his first 'trick'.
  5 The winner of the trick chooses another card to start playing for the next trick. The winner of this trick leads to the next and so on until all four tricks are won.
  Try playing with more cards (5 cards = 5 tricks, 6 cards = 6 tricks and so on).

Fig 29

- **Trumps**

  Trumps are played like *Tricks* (above), but one suit is chosen to
  be the 'trump' suit. Trumps can be chosen after dealing by
  turning over the next card and seeing what suit it is. Any card
  of the trump suit beats any other card except a higher trump.
  For example if hearts are trumps a 2 of hearts beats any dia-
  mond, club or spade card but is beaten by any higher heart eg
  3 of hearts. Players must still follow suit during play if they
  can, but can play a trump card if they do not have a card of
  that suit. If trumps are played the highest trump card wins
  that trick.

- **Whist**

  Whist is a game of *Trumps* played with 7 cards each. When two
  play the winner is the player who makes 4 tricks.

There are many variations of whist, the most interesting being
German Whist. Other great card games for older children include
Rummy and *Cribbage*.

Key skills: Playing by rules and strategic thinking.

116 More board games   *9 years–adult*

The most challenging board game for any child is chess. However there are many easier traditional board games that get children thinking. One of a family of games played all over the world is called *Fox and Geese* (or *Cows and Leopards* or *Shepherds and Wolf*)

- **Shepherds and wolf**
  The game is played on a chess board, with four white and one black piece (see fig 30).
  The Shepherds are put on the black squares at one end of the board, defending the sheepfold, while the Wolf can start on any black square. The Shepherds move forward one square at a time diagonally onto a vacant black square, as in *Draughts* – but cannot move backwards. The Wolf can only move one square in a diagonal, also on the black squares, but either forwards and backwards like a king in *Draughts*. Neither Shepherds nor Wolf can jump over or capture each other.
  1 The Shepherds have the first move.
  2 The Shepherds win the game if they can trap the wolf so that it cannot make a valid move (that is, two diagonal steps in any direction).
  3 The Wolf wins if it can get past the Shepherds and reach their end of the board (the sheepfold)..
  At the end of the game players swap roles and ends. Try playing the game when the Wolf can only move two squares diagonally at a time.

O O O O ●

Fig 30

- **Fox and geese**

   This game can be played on a chessboard (as above), a solitaire board or on the intersections of a special board. There are twelve white pieces (geese), which start on the first three rows of black squares – and one black piece (the fox) which starts on one of the black corner squares at the end of the board.

   The first player moves the fox, the other player moves the geese. The fox can move one square in any direction or jump over a goose if it is next to it. A goose that is jumped over is removed from the board. The fox must land in an empty square. A goose can only move forward or sideways, and cannot jump. If the fox eats so many geese it cannot be trapped then the fox wins. If the geese corner the fox, then the geese win the game.

On the board shown below there are 13 geese and one fox.

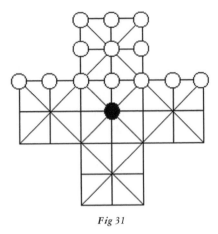

Fig 31

Key skills: Strategic thinking, planning and logical thinking

117 Secret numbers   *9 years–adult*

Being able to do maths in your head is an important skill so play
some mental maths games with your child.

- **Secret numbers**
  Secret numbers is a 'mind-reading' game that encourages logical deduction as well as an understanding of numbers. Any
  number of players can play and it takes no preparation.
  1 One player volunteers to think of a secret number
    between 0 and 100 (the player might be asked to write
    the number down, if there is any danger of forgetting it –
    or of cheating!)
  2 The other players have 10 questions to try to discover the
    secret number.
  3 The player with the secret number can only answer ques-
    tions with 'yes' or 'no'.
  4 The player who guesses the secret number within the 10

question limit wins and can start the next round. If no-one guesses the secret number the first player wins.

With a younger child try a lower limit, like 0–20 or 0–50. Once getting a secret number between 0–100 is easy, try 1–1000, then 1–10,000. Talk about which questions best help to narrow down possible answers – 'Is the number odd or even?' is a good one to start with.

Adapt the game to find a mystery animal, or any other 'secret' object and ask your child try to find what it is in as few questions as possible.

- **Think of a number**
  1 Say to your child 'Think of a secret number between 1 and 10. Double it. Add five Take away three. Halve it. Take away the number you first thought of. ' Give time for your child to make the calculations in his head (or write them down if he finds this too hard) Then tell him the answer he should have, which is seven. Try other 'think of a number puzzles, such as:
  2 Think of a number. Double it. Add the number you first thought of. Double it. Add the number you first thought of. Divide it be seven. The answer is the number you started with.
  3 Think of a number. Double it. Double it again. Add the number you first thought of. Divide it by five. Your answer is the number you started with.

The 'think of a number' formulas above are what mathematicians call 'algorithms'. See if you and your child can make up your own 'Think of a number' formulas.

Key skills: Mental maths, questioning and logical deduction.

118 The Great Panjandrum (or Poison Letter)
9 years–adult

This is a simple game for adults and children who can spell everyday words. It requires no equipment and can be played anywhere

- **The Great Panjandrum**

  1 For each round, one letter of the alphabet is chosen as the poison letter. Each player takes it in turns to choose the letter and to start the round by saying, 'The Great Panjandrum does not like the letter . . . What shall we . . .?' For example, *'The Great Panjandrum does not like the letter 'T'. What shall we give him to wear?'*

  2 Each player in turn tries to answer the question with words that do not include the poison letter. (In our example answers could include shoes, jumper, sandals, cap or sunglasses, but not trousers, shirt or hat since they contain the letter 'T'). Players must not repeat words that have been said and must answer within ten seconds of the previous answer. Any player who takes too long, cannot give a correct answer or gives an answer containing the poison letter is out for the rest of the round. Play continues until every player but one is out. The last player wins the round.

  3 The player who wins the round chooses the next poison letter and a question to ask. Some samples of questions are:
  What shall we give him to eat?
  What flowers does he like?
  What is his favourite colour?
  What did he do this morning?

  4 The overall winner is the player who wins most rounds, perhaps after every player has chosen a poison letter and question, or after an agreed time limit.

Key skills: Language and creative thinking.

119 Tangrams

9 years–adult

The tangram was invented in China and means 'seven boards of cunning'. It is a dissection puzzle consisting of seven flat shapes, called *tans*, which are put together to form shapes. The objective of the puzzle is to form a specific shape (given only in outline or silhouette) using all seven pieces, which may not overlap. It has become the most popular puzzle in the world and is easy to play with a commercial set or with pieces that you make yourself from card (see fig 32).

- **Tangram**
  The seven pieces make up a square, include five triangles, a rectangle (or trapezium) and a square. Using the seven pieces challenge your child to make an interesting shape. See below for some interesting shapes your child can make.

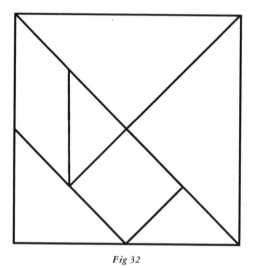

Fig 32

Key skills: Visual and problem solving skills

120 Tricky questions   *9 years–adult*

The world is full of interesting questions. Some of the most interesting questions may be the ones your child comes up with. Some of these tricky questions may be simple ones about how the world works ('empirical' questions) such as 'Why is the sky blue?' If your child asks such a question before you say – 'Look it up on Google' play the game of 'What might be a reason why?' If you have not time to discuss a tricky question that your child asks, tell him you will discuss it later. It is through asking questions that he finds out about the world and what he finds strange, interesting or puzzling about it. So try not to ignore his questions, otherwise he may stop asking them!

Some of your child's questions may be moral questions (about right and wrong) such as 'Is it ever right to kill people?' or controversial questions such as 'What happens when you die?' or 'Are there such things as ghosts?'

You can also challenge your child to think about some tricky questions, perhaps inspired by the stories you read together, films you see or TV programmes. Everyday life can also be a source of tricky questions, such as news stories, local problems or religious beliefs. You can introduce and discuss with your child some tricky questions at any time or place.

- **Tricky questions**
  Here are some tricky questions to think about with your child:
  1 How do you know you are not dreaming at this moment?
  2 How do you know when something is true or not true?
  3 Is an apple dead or alive?
  4 Is it right to eat animals?
  5 What is the difference between pretending and lying?
  6 What is the difference between a real person and a robot?
  7 Is there a difference between your mind and your brain?

8 Can animals think?
9 Is it ever right to tell lies?
10 What are the most valuable things in your life?

Fig 33

Key skills: Questioning, hypothesising, reasoning and creative thinking

Note:

For more on teaching children to think see Robert Fisher's website www.teachingthinking.net

Appendix

Travel games

On any long car trip with young children you'll be familiar with the cry, 'Are we there yet?' or one of its variations! Travel can get pretty boring for children when it takes for them what seems like hours. Here are some travel games that will engage bored minds.

1 Travel games for younger children

- **Lookout**
  Test the observation skills of players by getting them to look out for things.
  1 One player chooses an item for the other players to look out for. Examples might be: cows, umbrella, aeroplane, police officer, kind of bird, coach, red sports car, the number '7', a triangle, something purple etc.
  2 The first person to see the item gets one point.

3 The player with the highest score after a length of time eg 10 minutes wins the game.

- **What's my tune?**
  What's my tune? is a simple game that can be adapted to suit players of all ages.
  1 One player starts humming a song that everyone should know.
  2 When a player thinks they know what the tune is, they sing one or two bars of it. If they are correct, they get to choose another song to hum. If they are not right, the other players continue to try to guess the song.
  If your children are not very musical, you could pre-record a CD with about 20–30 songs they know. Players score one point for each song they can identify.

- **Letter spotting**
  Letter spotting is a game suitable for children of all ages. either individually or in pairs.
  1 The first player says a letter sound, for example if the letter is 'b' the sound to say would be 'ber' as in 'Can you see something beginning with 'ber'. The players then look for an object (inside or outside the car) beginning with that letter sound.
  2 The player who spots an obect, they chooses another letter or letter sound, such as 'p' or 'per' begin to look for the next object,

- **Alphabet spotting or I Spy A–Z**
  Players try to spot things beginning with each letter of the alphabet in turn from A–Z. For some of the harder letters eg 'q', 'u', 'x' and 'z', you could allow players to look for words which contain the letter rather than starting with that letter eg adverts, shop signs etc.

- **Five Senses Game**
  1 Name an object that you see while driving, for example, a tree, a cow, a tyre, etc.
  2 Ask your child describe it using the 5 senses: 'What does the object look like?', 'What sound does it make?' 'What would it taste like?' 'What does it smell like?' 'What is it like to touch?' This will encourage your child to think creatively and analytically about the things around him.

Other good travelling games for young children include:
- **I spy games:** (see also p62).
- **Memory games** such as *In my suitcase or My grandmother's cat* (p66).
- **Rhyming games** (p63).
- **Question games** (p54).

Key skills: Observation, language and sensory skills.

2 Travel games for older children

Number plate games can be played by any number of players. Try these three games:

- **Funny names**
  Funny names is a fun quick-thinking game for a family travelling in a car.
  1 Take the initials on the registration plate of any vehicle you can see.
  2 Using the letters, but ignoring the numbers, each player makes up a person's name using the initials in order. For example BPL could become 'Boris Patrick Lane' or 'Becky Paula Lincoln'.
  3 There are no winners or losers, though the winner could be the one who makes the most original name.

- **Silly sentences**

  Silly sentences is another fun game for quick thinkers.

  1 Take the initials on the registration plate of any vehicle you can see.

  2 Using the letters, and ignoring the numbers, each player makes up a phrase or sentence with words that begin with the letters on the number plate, for example 'BPC' might be 'Beware Pandas Crossing'. Players might choose some or all the letters on a plate to include in their phrase.

  3 There are no winners or losers, though the winner could be the one who makes the best silly sentence.

- **Make a word**

  Make a word is a more challenging game to play using car number plates.

  1 Each player looks for letters of a number plate on a vehicle they can see.

  2 Each then tries to think of a word that contains the letters of the registration plate, ignoring any numbers. The word must contain all the letters in their correct order, for example: BLO could be 'BLOw' or 'BaLlOon', CKN could be 'ChicKeN', and 'LPG' could be 'sLaPpinG'

  You could score one point for each letter of the word eg 'blow' would score 4 points, and 'chicken' 7 points. The winner is the player with the highest score.

- **Travel Hunt**

  For *Travel Hunt* you need to prepare a list of about 30 items for each player. The list could vary from player to player, and for the youngest pictures could be used instead of words.

  1 When each player sees an object on their list, they cross it off.

  2 The first player to finish their list wins.

Choose items you will see on your trip, for example: telegraph pole, supermarket, brick house, tractor, plane, horse, barn, pizza shop, bike, seagull, policeman, petrol station etc.

Other good travelling games for older children include:
- **Connect** (see p95) or **Disconnections** (see p153).
- **Questioning games** such as Twenty questions (see p92).
- **Memory games** (see p144).
- **What am I thinking of?** (p136).

Key skills: Observation and language skills.

Index of Brain Games